WHIMSICAL TREATS

ELF FOOD

ELF FOOD

85 HOLIDAY SWEETS & TREATS FOR A MAGICAL CHRISTMAS

CAYLA GALLAGHER

Skyhorse Publishing

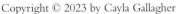

Skyhorse Publishing books may be purchased in bulk at special discounts for sales promotion, corporate gifts, fund-raising, or educational purposes. Special editions can also be created to specifications. For details, contact the Special Sales Department, Skyhorse Publishing, 307 West 36th Street, 11th Floor, New York, NY 10018 or info@skyhorsepublishing.com.

Skyhorse® and Skyhorse Publishing® are registered trademarks of Skyhorse Publishing, Inc.®, a Delaware corporation.

Visit our website at www.skyhorsepublishing.com.

10 9 8 7 6 5 4 3 2 1

Library of Congress Cataloging-in-Publication Data is available on file.

Cover design by David Ter-Avanesyan
Cover photo by Cayla Gallagher

Edited by Nicole Frail

Print ISBN: 978-1-5107-7697-5
Ebook ISBN: 978-1-5107-7698-2

Printed in China

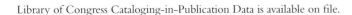

To my followers, a.k.a. my "bunnies." You have supported me through thick and thin, and I am endlessly appreciative of the opportunities that I have been given because of your support. I love every single one of you!

CONTENTS

INTRODUCTION

Welcome to my second Christmas cookbook, which I suppose you could call a sequel to *Reindeer Food*! I'm so excited to bring you even more holiday baking ideas and treats to enjoy by yourself or with family and friends. You'll also find a recipe for Gingerbread Cookies for Dogs (page 65), because our pups deserve to be included in the holiday festivities, as well!

  You'll find several classic recipes in this book, such as Classic Gingerbread Cookies (page 71), Snickerdoodles (page 60), and Hot Chocolate Bombs (page 135), as well as plenty of creative spins like my Red Velvet Gingerbread Cookies (page 72), Eggnog Hot Chocolate (page 132), and the cutest little Wreath Bagels (page 161). Prep for Christmas morning with my Christmas-Morning Oatmeal (page 167), enjoy some Strawberry Hot Chocolate (page 137) as you unwrap presents, and surprise everyone after Christmas dinner with Chicken Drumstick Cakes (page 17) and a funny story of *why* these are a holiday tradition in one part of the world! You'll also find plenty of Instagram-worthy cakes that will wow your guests but are actually super easy to make!

  It has been an absolute pleasure to write these books, and I am incredibly grateful for your support and enthusiasm. I wish you all a safe, happy, and wonderful holiday season and the best of luck with your holiday baking! If you have any questions along the way, please don't hesitate to reach out to me on social media!

Instagram: @pankobunny ❄ YouTube: @pankobunny ❄ Facebook: @pankobunnycooking

CAKES

Snowball Cake Pops

MAKES 12 (1-INCH) CAKE POPS

You'll much prefer to eat these snowballs rather than throw them! If you'd like to serve these on sticks, dip a lollipop stick into some extra melted white chocolate and insert it into each ball before you chill them in step 3.

Base:
4 vanilla cupcakes (3D Snowman Cupcakes, page 11)
¾ cup white chocolate chips, melted
¼ cup whipping cream
Pinch of salt

Coating:
½ cup sweetened coconut shavings
½ cup marshmallow bits
1 tablespoon edible glitter
2 cups white chocolate chips, melted

1. Place the cupcakes in a large bowl and break them apart until they are a fine crumb.

2. In a separate bowl, combine the melted white chocolate chips, whipping cream, and salt. Mix well. Add this to the cake crumbs and mix until fully combined. You can use an electric hand mixer if you like.

3. Divide the mixture into 12 and roll into balls. Place them on a plate lined with plastic wrap and chill in the fridge for about 30 minutes, or until firm.

4. To decorate, mix together the coconut shavings, marshmallow bits, and edible glitter in a bowl. Drop a cake pop into the melted white chocolate chips and scoop it up with a fork. Allow the excess chocolate to drip off, then drop it into the bowl with the toppings. Gently press the topping onto the top and sides of the cake pop, then return it to its plate.

5. Continue with the rest of the cake pops, then chill them again in the fridge for about 15 minutes or until the chocolate coating has set. Enjoy!

REINDEER CUPCAKES

MAKES 12 CUPCAKES

These reindeer cupcakes are extra happy because they're made with my favorite ultra-moist chocolate cupcake recipe and contain a cannoli filling!

Cupcake Batter:
1 cup all-purpose flour
1 cup granulated sugar
½ cup cocoa powder
1 teaspoon baking powder
¾ teaspoon baking soda
½ teaspoon salt
½ cup milk
¼ cup vegetable oil
1 large egg
1 teaspoon vanilla extract
½ cup boiling water

Filling:
½ cup ricotta cheese
½ cup mascarpone cheese
½ teaspoon vanilla extract
½ cup confectioners' sugar
⅓ cup mini chocolate chips

Buttercream:
2 cups unsalted butter, room temperature
2 teaspoons vanilla extract
½ cup milk
4 cups confectioners' sugar
1½ cups cocoa powder

Decorations:
24 pretzels
12 red candies
Black food coloring

Bake the Cupcakes:

1. Preheat the oven to 350°F and line a cupcake pan with cupcake liners.

2. Combine the flour, sugar, cocoa powder, baking powder, baking soda, and salt in a large bowl.

3. Add the milk, vegetable oil, egg, and vanilla extract, and mix with an electric mixer until combined. Slowly add the boiling water and mix until well combined.

4. Divide the batter evenly into the cupcake pan and bake for 20 to 25 minutes, until a skewer inserted into the cupcakes comes out clean. Cool completely.

Fill the Cupcakes:

1. Combine the ricotta cheese, mascarpone cheese, and vanilla extract in a bowl. Add the confectioners' sugar and mix until well combined. Then fold in the chocolate chips.

2. Use a spoon or the wide end of a piping tip to make a hole in the center of each of the cupcakes.

3. Place a generous dollop of filling into each hole.

Make the Buttercream:

1. Place the butter in a large bowl and beat with an electric mixer until pale and fluffy. Add the vanilla extract and milk and mix well.

(Continued on page 6)

2. Add the confectioners' sugar 1 cup at a time, beating with each addition. Then beat for 1 to 2 minutes, until light and fluffy.

3. Set aside ¼ cup of white buttercream. Add the cocoa powder to the remaining buttercream and mix until well combined.

Decorate the Cupcakes:

1. Place a generous dollop of chocolate buttercream onto a cupcake and smooth the surface so that the surface is flat and the edges of the buttercream are squared.

2. Use some pretzels to create antlers and a red candy as the nose. Place the white buttercream into a piping bag fitted with a small, round piping tip and pipe little white dots on the forehead.

3. Add some black food coloring to the remaining chocolate buttercream and place it in a piping bag fitted with a small, round piping tip. Pipe the smiling eyes!

CLEMENTINE CUPCAKES

MAKES 13 CUPCAKES

These cupcakes both look and taste exactly like fresh clementines!

Clementine Jam:
22 clementines, peeled (flesh and peel separated into bowls)
1½ cups granulated sugar

Cupcakes:
1½ cups + 2 tablespoons flour
1¼ cups sugar
¾ teaspoon baking soda
½ teaspoon baking powder
¾ teaspoon salt
1 egg + 1 egg yolk
⅔ cup water
⅔ cup buttermilk (or ⅔ cup milk and 2½ teaspoons white vinegar, combined and refrigerated for 15 minutes)
⅓ cup vegetable oil
1 teaspoon vanilla extract
Zest from 2 clementines
Dash of pure orange extract

Buttercream:
1 cup unsalted butter, room temperature
½ teaspoon vanilla extract
½ teaspoon pure orange extract
Zest from 1 clementine
3 cups confectioners' sugar
Orange food coloring

Decorations:
Orange sanding sugar
Pocky sticks (for stems)

Make the Jam:

1. Bring a pot of water to a boil and add about half of the clementine peels. Discard the remaining peels. Bring the water back up to a boil, then strain and let cool. Once cooled, slice the peels into 2-millimeter-thick strips.

2. Place the clementine flesh into a blender and pulse until smooth. Pour the blended clementine and sugar into a pot and bring it to a boil.

3. Remove any foam from the surface. Add the peel and simmer until the mixture reduces by two thirds. Pour the jam into a mason jar and cool.

Bake the Cupcakes:

1. Preheat the oven to 350°F and line a cupcake tin with cupcake liners.

2. Sift the flour, sugar, baking soda, baking powder, and salt in a bowl. Pour the dry ingredients into the bowl of an electric mixer and add the egg and egg yolk, water, buttermilk, oil, vanilla, clementine zest, and orange extract. Beat on low speed until fully combined, about 3 minutes.

3. Pour the mixture into the lined tin and bake for 20 minutes. Cool in the pan for 20 minutes, then transfer to a wire rack and cool completely.

(Continued on page 8)

Make the Buttercream:

1. Beat the butter in a bowl with an electric mixer until pale and fluffy. Add the vanilla extract, orange extract and clementine zest and mix well. Add the confectioners' sugar 1 cup at a time until fully combined. Add the orange food coloring and mix until fluffy.

Decorate the Cupcakes:

1. Make a hole in the center of each cupcake and fill it with jam. Mound some buttercream on top of each cupcake to look like a round clementine.

2. Pour the orange sanding sugar into a bowl and dunk each cupcake into the sugar, coating the entire surface of the buttercream in the sugar. Gently round the tops out with your hand if the buttercream gets misshapen. Stick a small piece of Pocky into the center to look like stems. Enjoy!

3D Snowman Cupcakes

MAKES 6 CUPCAKES

It's always perfect weather for snowmen in your kitchen! No hats or gloves required.

Cupcake Base:
2 cups all-purpose flour
3½ teaspoons baking powder
½ teaspoon salt
½ cup unsalted butter, room temperature
1 cup granulated sugar
1 teaspoon vanilla extract
1 teaspoon coconut extract
2 large eggs
1 cup milk

Buttercream:
2 cups unsalted butter, room temperature
1 teaspoon vanilla extract
5 cups confectioners' sugar

Decorations:
2 cups white chocolate chips, melted
2½ cups sweetened coconut shavings
30 mini chocolate chips
Orange food coloring
6 strips red licorice

Bake the Cupcakes:

1. Preheat the oven to 350°F. Line a cupcake pan with cupcake liners.

2. Combine the flour, baking powder, and salt. In a separate bowl, cream the butter and sugar with an electric mixer until pale and fluffy. Add the vanilla, coconut extract, and eggs and beat until combined. Add the dry mixture in two phases, alternating with the milk.

3. Divide the batter into the cupcake pan. Bake for 15 to 20 minutes, or until a skewer inserted into the centers comes out clean. Transfer to a wire rack and cool completely.

4. Take 6 of the cupcakes and use them to create a cake pop base (Snowball Cake Pops, page 3). Because the recipe on page 3 calls for 4 cupcakes instead of 6, you will need to increase the other ingredients by 50% to make the correct amount of pops for your snowman: use 1 cup of white chocolate chips and ⅓ cup whipping cream.

5. Make six small cake pops (1¼-inch diameter) and six medium cake pops (1¾-inch diameter). Place them on a plate lined with plastic wrap and chill for 30 minutes.

Make the Buttercream:

1. Cream the butter with an electric mixer until pale and fluffy. Add the vanilla extract and combine. Add the confectioners' sugar 1 cup at a time, then beat for 3 to 5 minutes until fluffy.

(Continued on page 12)

Decorate:

1. Drop a cake pop into the melted white chocolate chips and scoop it up with a fork. Allow the excess chocolate to drip off, then drop it into the coconut shavings. Gently roll it around to coat all sides, then return it to the plate. Repeat with all the cake pops, then place them in the fridge to chill for about 20 minutes, until the chocolate has set.

2. Spread some buttercream onto each cupcake and shape it into a round mound. Then dunk the cupcakes upside down into the coconut shavings, fully coating the buttercream.

3. Place a medium cake pop onto the center of each cupcake. Dip the base of a small cake pop in the excess melted white chocolate and stick it on top of the medium cake pop.

4. Use some extra buttercream to "glue" the mini chocolate chips to the snowmen, creating the eyes and buttons.

5. Add some orange food coloring to the remaining buttercream and place it in a piping bag fitted with a small, round piping tip. Pipe a carrot nose onto each snowman.

6. Drape a licorice scarf around each snowman and enjoy!

Hot Chocolate Cupcakes

MAKES 12 CUPCAKES

Rich, chocolaty, and delicious. These are hot chocolate in cake form!

Cupcake Batter:
1 cup all-purpose flour
1 cup granulated sugar
⅓ cup cocoa powder
¾ teaspoon baking soda
½ teaspoon salt
½ cup milk
¼ cup vegetable oil
1 large egg
1 teaspoon vanilla extract
½ cup boiling water

Ganache Frosting:
12 ounces semisweet chocolate, finely
  chopped
1½ cups whipping cream
Pinch of salt
1 teaspoon vanilla extract

Decorations:
5 pieces white taffy candy (Airheads, for
  example)
White sprinkles
½ cup marshmallow fluff
12 chocolate/brown candy cane sticks
12 squares chocolate
⅓ cup marshmallow bits

Bake the Cupcakes:

1. Preheat the oven to 350°F. Line a cupcake pan with liners and set aside.

2. Place the flour, sugar, cocoa powder, baking powder, and salt in a large bowl and mix well.

3. Add the milk, vegetable oil, egg, and vanilla extract and mix well. Add the boiling water and mix until well combined.

4. Pour the mixture into the cupcake pan. Bake for 20 to 30 minutes, until a skewer inserted into the middle comes out clean. Cool completely.

Make the Frosting:

1. Place the chocolate into a large bowl and set aside.

2. Pour the whipping cream into a small pot and set it to medium-high heat. Heat until it just starts to bubble. Pour the cream directly onto the chocolate and let stand for 5 minutes.

3. Add the salt and vanilla extract, then whisk to combine. Allow the ganache to set at room temperature for 2 hours, or until it has the same consistency as buttercream frosting.

4. Beat the ganache with an electric mixer for just a couple minutes until it becomes light, fluffy, and holds stiff peaks. Place the ganache in a piping bag fitted with a large, star-shaped piping tip. Set aside.

(Continued on page 14)

Make the Mini Mugs:

1. Use your hands to shape the taffy into little bowl shapes. Roll some extra taffy into long sausages and stick them onto the sides of the bowls to look like handles. The warmth of your hands should be enough for the handles to stick.

2. Take some extra ganache frosting and fill the mugs to look like hot chocolate! Add some white sprinkles on top.

Decorate the Cupcakes:

1. Place the marshmallow fluff into a piping bag and snip off the end to create a medium-sized hole. Pipe a dollop of marshmallow fluff onto the center of each cupcake.

2. Pipe the ganache frosting in a swirl onto the cupcakes, so that the marshmallow dollop is in the center of the frosting swirl.

3. Top each cupcake with a candy cane stick, a square of chocolate, a sprinkle of marshmallow bits, and a mini hot chocolate mug. Enjoy!

Chicken Drumstick Cakes

It might seem odd for this recipe to be in a Christmas cookbook, but in Japan, fried chicken is actually a very popular Christmas Day dinner! So popular, in fact, that families preorder their fried chicken in November. Serve a drumstick along with your other desserts for a fun, Japanese twist on Christmas!

Base:
1½ cups white chocolate chips
½ cup whipping cream
8 chocolate cupcakes, crumbled (Reindeer Cupcakes, page 5)

Coating:
3 cups white chocolate chips, melted
2–3 cups cornflakes, crushed

Make the Base:

1. In a small pot, heat the white chocolate chips and whipping cream over low heat until the chocolate has melted and is combined with the cream.

2. Pour the chocolate and cream mixture into the cake crumbs created from the base of the Reindeer Cupcakes recipe on page 5 and mix everything together. Divide the mixture into 9 portions.

3. Shape each portion into a drumstick shape and place them on a tray lined with plastic wrap. Place the tray in the freezer for 15 to 20 minutes until they stiffen.

Decorate:

1. One by one, coat the drumsticks in the melted white chocolate and dunk them directly into the crushed cornflakes. Once they are fully coated, place them on a tray lined with parchment paper. Place them in the fridge until the chocolate has hardened, about 20 minutes.

2. For a fun presentation, place them in an empty fried chicken bucket if you have one handy and enjoy!

ELF CAKE

MAKES 1 (6-INCH) CAKE

The cutest, most festive elf cake! This might seem intimidating—especially that hat!—but it's actually very easy with the help of crispy rice cereal! This allows you to create shapes you normally can't with cake and, as someone who is not a big fan of fondant, this is my favorite way to create those shapes while still maintaining a delicious cake!

Cake Base:
Cooking spray
1 cup unsalted butter, room temperature
2 cups granulated sugar
3 teaspoons vanilla extract
6 large eggs, room temperature
3 cups all-purpose flour
1 teaspoon baking soda
1 teaspoon salt
1½ cups sour cream
Red food coloring

Buttercream:
2 cups unsalted butter, room temperature
1 teaspoon vanilla extract
5 cups confectioners' sugar

Hat Base:
¼ cup unsalted butter
5 cups mini marshmallows
1 teaspoon vanilla extract
4 cups crispy rice cereal
1½ cups melted candy wafers
3 lollipop sticks (if you have the choice
    between long or short sticks, choose long!)
¾ cup white and gold sprinkles
Orange, brown, red, and green food
    coloring

Bake the Cake:

1. Grease and flour 3 (6-inch) round cake pans and preheat the oven to 350°F.

2. Beat the butter and sugar with an electric mixer until pale and smooth. Add the vanilla extract and eggs one at a time, mixing with each addition.

3. In a separate bowl, combine the flour, baking soda, and salt. Add this to the batter in two phases, alternating with the sour cream.

4. Divide the batter into two bowls. Dye one bowl red and leave the other bowl white.

5. Dollop large spoonfuls of both colors of batter into both pans so that you have a polka-dot effect. Take a butter knife and gently swirl it through the batter a couple of times to create a marble effect.

6. Bake for 50 to 60 minutes, or until a skewer inserted into the center of the cakes comes out clean. Cool completely.

Make the Buttercream:

1. Place the butter in a large bowl and beat with an electric mixer until pale and fluffy. Add the vanilla extract and mix to combine.

2. Add the confectioners' sugar 1 cup at a time, mixing with each addition. Then beat for another 3 minutes, until light and fluffy.

(Continued on page 20)

Assembly:

1. Cut the tops and bottoms off the cakes to create flat surfaces.

2. Place one cake on your work surface and dollop ½ cup of buttercream on top and spread it to the edges of the cake. Place another layer of cake on top and repeat with another ½ cup buttercream.

3. Place the third layer of cake on top and cover the cake in a thin, even layer of buttercream. Transfer the cake to the fridge to chill for 15 minutes while you make the hat base.

Make the Hat base:

1. Melt the butter in a pot over low heat. Add the mini marshmallows and mix until fully melted. Remove from the heat and add the vanilla extract. Add the crispy rice cereal and mix well.

2. Allow the mixture to cool until it is easily handled. Spray your hands with cooking spray and shape some of the mixture into a 2-inch-diameter ball. Insert one of the lollipop sticks into the ball and set aside on a plate lined with plastic wrap.

3. Use the remaining mixture to create the elf's hat! Gently add it to the top of the cake, first creating a pyramid, then slowly adding more to create the loop of the hat. To make it look natural, make sure that the loop of the hat tapers in thickness toward the end. The trim of the hat is made out of buttercream, so don't worry about that part yet! Place the cake in the fridge while you make the ears.

Make the Ears:

1. Place a sheet on parchment paper onto a flat tray that will fit into your fridge.

2. Place two dollops of melted candy wafers onto the parchment and place a lollipop stick onto each dollop.

3. The lollipop stick will act as a "bone" to provide strength for the ears, as well as a way to attach them to the cake!

4. Spread more candy wafers on top, creating your desired shape of the ears. Don't be shy about creating a thick layer, as this will make them more sturdy and less likely to break.

5. Once you are satisfied with the shapes of the ears, place the tray in the fridge for the candy wafers to harden.

Make the Pompom:

1. Take the crispy rice cereal ball and coat it in the remaining melted candy wafers.

2. While the candy wafers are still wet, roll the ball in the white and gold sprinkles, gently pressing them onto the ball with your hands.

3. Return the ball, with the lollipop stick still attached, to its place and chill it in the fridge until needed.

Decorate the Cake:

1. Place about ½ of the buttercream in a bowl. Add some orange and brown food coloring to create your desired skin tone. You will only need a fraction of a drop of each color.

2. Spread this buttercream onto the sides of the cake (not the top!). Then stick the ears into the sides of the cake and gently cover the ears in an even layer of buttercream.

3. Add several more drops of brown food coloring to the remaining skin-tone buttercream to create the elf's hair! Then place this buttercream into a piping bag fitted with a medium-sized, round piping tip.

4. Pipe tufts of the elf's hair all around the sides of the cake, leaving space for where his face will be. Use a similar technique to applying shingles on a house—work in layers, starting at the bottom. This will make the hair look natural!

5. Place the remaining brown buttercream into a piping bag fitted with a small, round piping tip and pipe the elf's eyes onto the cake.

6. Divide the remaining buttercream in half. Dye one half green. Use that green buttercream for the hat, covering it with a smooth, even layer. To the remaining green buttercream, add a dollop of white buttercream and mix it just once or twice. Then spoon it into a piping bag fitted with a medium-sized, round piping tip. Set aside.

7. Dye the remaining buttercream red and place it in a piping bag fitted with a small, round piping tip. Pipe the elf's cheeks onto its face and use a knife to smooth them out and create flat circles.

8. With the remaining red buttercream, pipe designs onto the elf's hat. You can use a toothpick to etch your design into the green buttercream first, to create a template for yourself. Then simply pipe the red buttercream on top!

9. Take the green and white piping bag from step 6 and pipe the trim of the hat onto the cake, making many little dollops. Decorate the trim with the remaining white and gold sprinkles.

10. Lastly, stick the pompom onto the cake, using the lollipop stick as an anchor. Enjoy your little elf!

Jumbo Ornament Cake

SERVES 6-8

This is my favorite vanilla cake, but with a twist! I added some melted butterscotch chips directly to the cake batter, which gives the cake a boost of moisture and adds an insanely delicious warmth to the flavor of the cake.

Cake Base:

1 cup unsalted butter, room temperature
2 cups granulated sugar
3 teaspoon vanilla extract
6 large eggs, room temperature
3 cups all-purpose flour
1 teaspoon baking soda
1 teaspoon salt
1½ cups sour cream
1 cup butterscotch chips (not toffee chips), melted
Cooking spray, for cake pans

Buttercream:

2 cups unsalted butter, room temperature
1 teaspoon vanilla extract
5 cups confectioners' sugar

Decoration:

1 peanut butter cup
Silver edible food spray
1 tiny piece of fondant
Black food coloring

Bake the Cake:

1. Grease and flour 3 (6-inch) round cake pans and preheat the oven to 350°F.

2. Beat the butter and sugar with an electric mixer until pale and smooth. Add the vanilla extract and eggs one at a time, mixing with each addition.

3. In a separate bowl, combine the flour, baking soda, and salt. Add this to the batter in two phases, alternating with the sour cream. Then add the melted butterscotch chips and mix until combined.

4. Divide the batter between the pans and bake for 40 to 50 minutes, or until a skewer inserted into the center of the cakes comes out clean. Cool completely.

Make the Buttercream:

1. Place the butter in a large bowl and beat with an electric mixer until pale and fluffy. Add the vanilla extract and mix to combine.

2. Add the confectioners' sugar 1 cup at a time, mixing with each addition. Then beat for another 3 minutes, until light and fluffy.

Decorations:

1. Place the peanut butter cup on a sheet of parchment paper and spray it with the silver edible food spray. Roll the fondant into a small sausage, shape it into an upside-down U-shape, and stick it on top of the peanut butter cup. Spray it with another coat of silver food spray. Allow this to dry while you assemble the cake.

(Continued on page 24)

Assembly:

1. Slice the bottoms off all the cakes to remove any excess browning. Slice the tops off two of the cakes, leaving the roundest cake with the top intact. This will help you shape the cake!

2. Stack the cakes, spreading ½ cup of buttercream between each layer. The cake with the intact top should be at the top of the stack.

3. Use a serrated knife to carve the cake into a spherical shape. Don't worry about the cake scraps! You can use them for cake pops!

4. Cover the cake in a thin, even layer of buttercream. This will trap all the crumbs and prevent them from showing on the outside of the cake. Place the cake in the fridge for 15 minutes, so that this layer can stiffen.

5. Coat the cake in a thick, generous layer of buttercream. Smooth out the surface as much as possible, like an ornament!

6. Dye the remaining buttercream black with the black food coloring. Place the buttercream into a piping bag fitted with a small, round piping tip. Pipe snowflakes all over the cake.

7. Gently place the peanut butter cup on top and enjoy!

CHRISTMAS PRESENT CAKE

SERVES 9–10

What better present is there other than one made of sugar and butter?!

Cake Batter:
Cooking spray, for greasing the cake pans
2 cups all-purpose flour
2 cups granulated sugar
¾ cup cocoa powder
2 teaspoons baking powder
1½ teaspoons baking soda
1 teaspoon salt
1 cup milk
½ cup vegetable oil
2 large eggs
2 teaspoons vanilla extract
1 cup boiling water

Bow:
10 ounces red fondant

Buttercream:
2 cups unsalted butter, room temperature
1 teaspoon vanilla extract
5 cups confectioners' sugar
½ cup raspberry jam, warmed
1 cup fresh raspberries
Red and green food coloring

Bake the Cake:

1. Grease and flour 3 (6-inch) square cake pans, and preheat the oven to 350°F.

2. Place the flour, sugar, cocoa powder, baking powder, baking soda, and salt in a large bowl and mix together.

3. Add the milk, vegetable oil, eggs, and vanilla extract and mix with an electric mixer until combined. Slowly add the boiling water and mix until well combined.

4. Divide the batter between the cake pans and bake for 30 to 35 minutes, until a skewer inserted into the center of the cakes comes out clean. Cool completely.

Make the Bow:

1. Divide the fondant into 3 pieces. Wrap 2 pieces in plastic wrap and set aside for later.

2. Divide the remaining piece into 4 pieces. First, make the loops of the bow by rolling 2 of the pieces into 2 × 6–inch strips. Wrap these around a narrow bottle, or anything that will allow each strip to form a loop shape and the ends to be pinched together. Place these on a baking sheet lined with plastic wrap.

3. Roll out the remaining 2 pieces into 1½ × 4–inch strips. Cut notches into one end of each strip. This will create the "tails" of the bow. Place these on that same baking sheet. You can place little balls of crumpled aluminum foil underneath these tails to create ripples in the ribbon.

(Continued on page 26)

4. Set this tray aside and allow the fondant to harden while you build the cake.

Make the Buttercream:
1. Place the butter into a large bowl and beat with an electric mixer until pale and fluffy. Add the vanilla extract and mix until combined.

2. Add the confectioners' sugar 1 cup at a time, beating with each addition. Beat the buttercream for an additional 3 minutes, until fluffy.

Assembly:
1. Place one cake on your work surface and brush the surface with half of the raspberry jam.

2. Spread ½ cup of buttercream onto the cake and scatter half of the raspberries on top. Place another layer of cake on top and repeat with the raspberry jam, buttercream, and raspberries.

3. Place the third layer of cake on top and cover the cake in a thin, even layer of buttercream. Place the cake in the fridge for 15 minutes to chill.

4. Cover the cake in a thick, smooth layer of buttercream, sharpening the edges to keep them square.

5. Roll the remaining 2 pieces of fondant into two 1½ × 20–inch strips. Drape them onto the cake, creating the ribbons that wrap around the cake. Roll any offcuts of the fondant into a ball and save for step 7.

6. Dye ½ cup of the remaining buttercream green and place it into a piping bag fitted with a small, leaf-shaped piping tip. Pipe holly leaves all over the cake. Dye ¼ cup of the remaining buttercream red and place it into a piping bag fitted with a small, round piping tip. Pipe red berries in the center of the holly leaves.

7. Place the tails of the ribbon onto the center of the cake, then place the loops on top. Take the excess fondant from step 5 and wrap it around the center of the loops to form the middle of the bow.

8. Slice and enjoy!

Snowy Forest Cabin Cake

SERVES 6-8

A black forest cake with a snowy twist! This is my favorite cake in this book. I think it looks so cozy and really captures the beauty of winter!

Syrup:
1 recipe Simple Syrup, still warm and in the pot (Simple Syrup, page 95)
1 cup frozen cherries, defrosted

Cake Batter:
Cooking spray
2 cups all-purpose flour
2 cups granulated sugar
¾ cup cocoa powder
2 teaspoons baking powder
1½ teaspoon baking soda
1 teaspoon salt
1 cup milk
½ cup vegetable oil
2 large eggs
2 teaspoons vanilla extract
1 cup boiling water

Trees:
½ cup chocolate chips, melted
3–4 Pocky sticks
1 Mini Gingerbread House (page 189)

Frosting:
3 cups whipping cream, cold
¼ cup confectioners' sugar, plus extra for the "snow"
2 teaspoons vanilla extract

Make the Syrup:

1. To the Simple Syrup recipe, add the defrosted cherries. Bring to a simmer, cover, and simmer for 10 minutes.

2. Turn off the heat and allow the cherries to steep in the syrup for 1 hour.

Bake the Cake:

1. Preheat the oven to 350°F and grease and flour 3 (6-inch) round baking pans.

2. Place the flour, sugar, cocoa powder, baking powder, baking soda, and salt in a large bowl and mix together.

3. Add the milk, vegetable oil, eggs, and vanilla extract and mix until well combined.

4. Divide the batter between the cake pans and bake for 30 to 35 minutes, until a skewer inserted into the cakes comes out clean. Cool completely.

Make the Trees:

1. Place the melted chocolate chips into a piping bag. You can simply snip off the end to create a small hole, or attach a small, star-shaped piping tip for added texture to the trees.

2. Line a tray with parchment paper. This tray should be small enough to fit into your fridge. Place the Pocky 1 to 2 inches apart.

(Continued on page 30)

3. Pipe the chocolate in a zigzag motion onto the Pocky, creating trees! You can make narrow trees, wide trees, short trees—anything!

4. Place the tray into the fridge to chill while you finish the cake.

Make the Frosting:
1. Pour the cream, confectioners' sugar, and vanilla extract into a large bowl and beat with an electric mixer, on medium-high speed, until stiff peaks form.

Assembly:
1. Cut the tops off the cakes so that they have a flat surface. Then brush a generous amount of cherry syrup onto the surfaces of the cakes.

2. Place one cake on your desired surface or cake stand. Spread about ½ cup of frosting onto the cake. Scatter 5 or 6 cherries from the cherry syrup on top.

3. Snack another cake on top and repeat with the frosting and cherries.

4. Place the final cake on top. Cover the entire cake in a thin layer of frosting. This style is called a Naked Cake and is done by gliding the spatula directly against the sides of the cake so that the frosting gets into the crevices and layers, but the sides stay mostly bare.

5. Add a large dollop of frosting on top of the cake and gently spread it to the edges, to look like a fresh snowfall.

6. Place the Mini Gingerbread House on top and stick the Pocky trees around the house. If desired, place the extra confectioners' sugar into a mesh sieve (or a tea strainer!) and dust a sprinkle of sugar onto the trees and house like snow.

Nutcracker Cake

SERVES 6-8

So charming and whimsical, this nutcracker is a vanilla cake with a fruit cake twist! Using only the delicious parts of fruit cake, I promise! I also felt obligated to add walnuts because what is a nutcracker without nuts?!

Cake Base:
Cooking spray, for cake pans
1 cup unsalted butter, room temperature
2 cups granulated sugar
3 teaspoons vanilla extract
6 large eggs, room temperature
3 cups all-purpose flour
1 teaspoon baking soda
1 teaspoon salt
1½ cups sour cream
½ cup chopped walnuts
½ cup chopped glacé (candied) cherries
½ cup chopped dried apricots
½ cup mini chocolate chips

Buttercream:
2 cups unsalted butter, room temperature
1 teaspoon vanilla extract
5 cups confectioners' sugar
½ cup apricot jam, warm
½ cup raw walnuts, roughly chopped
Orange, brown, black, red, and yellow food coloring

Bake the Cake:

1. Grease and flour 3 (6-inch) round cake pans and preheat the oven to 350°F.

2. Beat the butter and sugar with an electric mixer until pale and smooth. Add the vanilla extract and eggs one at a time, mixing with each addition.

3. In a separate bowl, combine the flour, baking soda, and salt. Add this to the batter in two phases, alternating with the sour cream.

4. Add the walnuts, glacé cherries, dried apricots, and mini chocolate chips and mix until just combined.

5. Divide the batter between the pans and bake for 50 to 60 minutes, or until a skewer inserted into the center of the cakes comes out clean. Cool completely.

Make the Buttercream:

1. Place the butter in a large bowl and beat with an electric mixer until pale and fluffy. Add the vanilla extract and mix to combine.

2. Add the confectioners' sugar 1 cup at a time, mixing with each addition. Then beat for another 3 minutes, until light and fluffy.

Assembly:

1. Cut the tops and bottoms off the cakes to create flat surfaces.

(Continued on page 32)

2. Place one cake on your work surface and brush the surface with the apricot jam. Dollop ½ cup of buttercream on top and spread it to the edges of the cake. Sprinkle half of the walnuts on top. Place another layer of cake on top and repeat with the jam, buttercream, and nuts.

3. Place the third layer of cake on top and cover the cake in a thin, even layer of buttercream. Transfer the cake to the fridge to chill for 15 minutes.

4. Place ½ cup of buttercream into a bowl and use the orange and brown food coloring to create the nutcracker's skin color. Use a very tiny amount of each—the brown with give you the skin tone and the orange will add warmth to the skin. I used about ⅛ of a drop of each. Spread this onto the bottom third of the cake, just where the face will be seen.

5. Dye ¼ cup of buttercream black and place it in a piping bag fitted with a large, round piping tip. Pipe 2 large dollops onto the face, creating the nutcracker's eyes.

6. Dye 1½ cups of buttercream red. Spread an even layer over the entire top two thirds of the cake, as well as the flat top of the cake. This will be his hat.

7. Fill a piping bag with some white buttercream and attach a large, round piping tip. Pipe the nutcracker's moustache in two flourishes, starting from the center and making one flourish toward the right, then one toward the left. Then pipe his hair around the perimeter of the bottom third of the cake, making squiggle shapes with the white buttercream.

8. Place some remaining white buttercream into a piping bag and snip off the end, creating a small hole. Pipe a dot on each eye, adding a sparkle! This gives so much life and personality to the cake.

9. Dye the remaining buttercream yellow and place it in a piping bag fitted with a medium-sized, round piping tip. Pipe the border of the hat, as well as the accents and buttons.

10. Enjoy your adorable nut-filled nutcracker!

CHOCOLATE ORANGE CHEESECAKE

MAKES 1 (9-INCH) CHEESECAKE

I love chocolate and orange during the holidays, and this cheesecake is so deliciously festive! It features homemade candied oranges, which, if you have leftovers, I recommend chopping up and folding into the buttercream filling of the Nutcracker Cake (page 31)!

Cheesecake Base:
14 ounces chocolate wafers, finely crushed
¼ cup unsalted butter, melted
Zest from 1 orange

Filling:
28 ounces cream cheese, room temperature
8 ounces semisweet chocolate, melted
Zest from 1 orange
¾ cup granulated sugar
¼ cup cocoa powder
800 milliliters whipping cream
Juice from 1 lemon
1 teaspoon vanilla extract
5 teaspoons powdered gelatin
5 tablespoons water

Topping:
½ orange, thinly sliced
½ cup sugar
¼ cup water
Gold sprinkles

Make the Base:
1. Combine the chocolate wafers, butter, and orange zest in a bowl.

2. Press it into the bottom of a 9-inch-round springform pan. Place the pan in the fridge to chill while you make the filling.

Make the Filling:
1. Beat the cream cheese with an electric mixer until smooth. Add the semisweet chocolate, orange zest, sugar, and cocoa powder and mix to combine.

2. Add the whipping cream, lemon juice, and vanilla extract and mix until combined.

3. Combine the gelatin and water in a small bowl and microwave for 30 seconds, or until the gelatin has fully melted. Add this to the cheesecake mixture and mix well until combined.

4. Pour into the springform pan and smooth the surface. Place in the fridge overnight, or until firm.

Make the Topping and Decorate:
1. Place the orange slices in a pot of cold water. Bring to a boil and boil for 30 seconds. Drain, then place in another pot with the sugar and 2 tablespoons water. Bring to a simmer and cook until the orange peel is translucent, 10 to 20 minutes.

2. Transfer to a plate and cool completely.

3. Slide a sharp knife around the inside edges of the cake pan, then release the sides of the pan.

4. Sprinkle a variety of gold sprinkles onto the cheesecake. Top with the candied oranges and enjoy!

GINGERBREAD MAN CAKE

SERVES 8-10

The most adorable holiday cake! This gingerbread man is feeling extra festive with the addition of juicy, citrusy cranberries and ginger jam.

Soaked Berries:
1 cup dried cranberries
1 cup orange juice

Cake Batter:
2 cups all-purpose flour
2 cups sugar
¾ cup cocoa powder + extra for dusting
    the pan
2 teaspoons baking powder
1½ teaspoons baking soda
1–2 tablespoons Gingerbread Spice Mix
    (page 93)
1 teaspoon salt
1 cup milk
½ cup vegetable oil
2 large eggs
2 teaspoons vanilla extract
1 cup boiling water

Buttercream:
2 cups unsalted butter, room temperature
2 teaspoons vanilla extract
1 tablespoon Gingerbread Spice Mix
    (page 93)
5 cups confectioners' sugar
2 tablespoons cocoa powder
Brown food coloring
¼ cup ginger jam
Peppermint candies

Make the Soaked Berries:

1. Pour the dried cranberries and orange juice into a bowl.

2. Cover with plastic wrap and refrigerate until ready to use. (I soaked mine for 1 full day. The longer you soak, the stronger they will taste.)

Bake the Cake:

1. Preheat the oven to 350°F. Grease and flour a 9 × 13–inch cake pan.

2. Place the flour, sugar, cocoa powder, baking powder, baking soda, Gingerbread Spice Mix, and salt in a large bowl and mix together.

3. Add the milk, vegetable oil, eggs, and vanilla extract and mix with an electric mixer until combined.

4. Slowly add the boiling water and mix until well combined.

5. Pour the batter into the pan and bake for 40 to 45 minutes, until a skewer inserted into the center comes out clean. Cool for 15 minutes in the pan, then turn onto a wire rack and cool completely.

Make the Buttercream:

1. Beat the butter with an electric mixer until pale and fluffy. Add the vanilla extract and Gingerbread Spice Mix and mix well. Add the confectioners' sugar 1 cup at a time, beating with each addition.

(Continued on page 38)

2. Place about 1½ cups of buttercream into a piping bag fitted with a medium-sized round piping tip.

3. To the remaining buttercream, add the cocoa powder and brown food coloring and mix well.

Assembly:

1. Slice the cake into two halves. Stack the halves on top of each other and carve them into a gingerbread man shape. Carefully remove the top layer and set aside.

2. Pipe three quarters of the white buttercream onto the bottom layer of cake. Use a cake spatula to smooth the frosting.

3. Drain the cranberries and discard (or drink!) the orange juice. Scatter the cranberries onto the white buttercream, along with dollops of ginger jam.

4. Place the remaining cake layer on top. Cover the entire cake in a thick, generous layer of brown buttercream.

5. Pipe a border, a face, squiggly lines, and buttons onto the gingerbread man with the remaining white buttercream. Stick peppermint candies onto the buttons, and enjoy!

RAINBOW YULE LOG CAKE

A fun, colorful take on a Christmas classic! Slice into this snowy white yule log to discover a swirl of rainbow hidden inside!

Cake Batter:
6 large eggs, yolks and white separated
Pinch salt
1 cup sugar
2 teaspoons vanilla extract
5 tablespoons unsalted butter, melted and cooled
1 cup all-purpose flour
Pink, orange, yellow, green, and blue food coloring
Confectioners' sugar, for dusting

Filling:
3 cups whipping cream, cold
¼ cup confectioners' sugar
2 teaspoons vanilla extract
Rainbow sprinkles

Make the Cake Batter:

1. Preheat the oven to 350°F and line a Swiss roll pan with parchment paper.

2. In a large bowl, beat the 6 egg whites and salt with an electric mixer until soft peaks form. Add half of the sugar and beat until stiff, glossy peaks form.

3. In a separate bowl, beat the egg yolks and remaining sugar with an electric mixer until pale and doubled in volume. Gradually add the vanilla extract and butter and mix until well combined.

4. Add the flour to the batter in two phases, alternating with the egg whites. Divide the batter into five bowls and dye them pink, orange, yellow, green, and blue. Make sure to very gently fold the food coloring into the batter, as you don't want to remove any air from the batter. Spoon the batter into piping bags and snip off the ends, creating a medium-sized hole in each bag.

5. Pipe diagonal stripes into the pan in the order of the rainbow. This will ensure that every slice will look like a rainbow! Bake for 13 to 15 minutes, until the edges are golden.

6. Dust a large sheet of wax paper with confectioners' sugar. As soon as the cake comes out of the oven, invert it onto the wax paper. Peel off the top layer of parchment paper, place another layer of wax paper on top, then invert again, so that the patterned side is

(Continued on page 40)

facing down. Remove the wax paper and starting at one long end, gently roll the cake up. Wrap in a kitchen towel and cool completely.

Make the Filling:

1. Beat the whipping cream with an electric mixer until soft peaks form. Add the confectioners' sugar and vanilla extract and beat until stiff peaks form.

Assembly:

1. Gently unroll the cake and peel off the wax paper. Spread the filling onto the inside and roll the cake back up again.

2. Wrap the cake in plastic wrap and chill in the fridge for 4 hours, or up to overnight.

3. Unwrap the cake and use a serrated knife to slice off the ends of the cake. Slice the cake into a 9-inch log and place this log on your serving platter. Slice the remaining, smaller log in half diagonally. This will create the two "stumps."

4. Cover all but the ends of the log in a thin, even layer of frosting. Stick the stumps onto the cake, using toothpicks to attach them if necessary. Then cover the cake in a thicker, generous layer of frosting.

5. Use a fork to create grooves in the frosting to resemble the bark of a log. Scatter some rainbow sprinkles on top and enjoy!

Santa Cake

SERVES 8-10

This cake is as delicious as it is cute! This is a white chocolate red velvet cake, where white chocolate is used in place of cocoa powder in the cake batter. It's topped with my absolute favorite cream cheese frosting. I'm always happy when I'm making a red velvet cake, simply because it's a great excuse to make this frosting and lick the bowl afterward!

Cake Base:
Cooking spray, for cake pans
1 cup unsalted butter, room temperature
2 cups granulated sugar
3 teaspoons vanilla extract
6 large eggs, room temperature
3 cups all-purpose flour
1 teaspoon baking soda
1 teaspoon salt
1½ cups sour cream
1 cup melted white chocolate
Red food coloring

Cream Cheese Frosting:
24 ounces cream cheese, room temperature
1½ cups unsalted butter, room temperature
2 teaspoons vanilla extract
9 cups confectioners' sugar
Orange, brown, black, and red food coloring
Red sugar sprinkles

Bake the Cake:

1. Grease and flour 3 (6-inch) round cake pans and preheat the oven to 350°F.

2. Beat the butter and sugar with an electric mixer until pale and smooth. Add the vanilla extract and eggs one at a time, mixing with each addition.

3. In a separate bowl, combine the flour, baking soda, and salt. Add this to the batter in two phases, alternating with the sour cream. Add the white chocolate and mix well. Dye the batter bright red with the red food coloring.

4. Divide the batter between the pans and bake for 50 to 60 minutes, or until a skewer inserted into the center of the cakes comes out clean. Cool completely.

Make the Frosting:

1. Place the cream cheese and butter in a large bowl and beat with an electric mixer until pale and fluffy. Add the vanilla extract and mix to combine.

2. Add the confectioners' sugar 1 cup at a time, mixing with each addition. Then beat for another 3 minutes, until light and fluffy.

Assembly:

1. Cut the tops and bottoms off the cakes to create flat surfaces.

(Continued on page 44)

2. Place one cake on your work surface and dollop ½ cup of frosting on top. Spread it to the edges of the cake. Place another layer of cake on top and repeat with the frosting.

3. Place the third layer of cake on top and cover the cake in a thin, even layer of frosting. Transfer the cake to the fridge to chill for 15 minutes.

4. Place ½ cup of frosting into a bowl and use the orange and brown food coloring to create the skin color. Use a very tiny amount of each—the brown will give you the skin tone and the orange will add warmth to the skin. I used about ¼ of a drop of each. Spread this onto the middle of the cake, just where the face will be seen.

5. Fill a piping bag with white frosting and attach a large, round piping tip. Pipe dollops of frosting onto the bottom two thirds of the cake, framing the face and creating Santa's beard and hair. Then pipe a flourish of frosting onto the middle of his face, creating his moustache!

6. Dye two thirds of the remaining frosting red. Place it into a piping bag fitted with a large, star-shaped piping tip. Pipe two rows around the top third of the cake, as well as the flat top of the cake. Don't make the long portion of the hat yet!

7. Place the remaining white frosting into a piping bag fitted with a large, star-shaped piping tip. This piping tip should be a different star shape than the red frosting. We want to add a different texture to this frosting, as we'll be piping large dollops around the edge of the hat, creating the hat's fluffy trim. Set this piping bag aside.

8. Using the same red frosting and piping tip, pipe the cascading hat down the side of the cake. Use large dollops to add height. Using the piping bag from step 7, pipe a large white dollop as the end of the hat as the pompom.

9. Dye one quarter of the remaining frosting (it can be the red or white frosting—both work!) black with the black food coloring. Place it into a piping bag fitted with a small, round piping tip. Pipe Santa's eyes onto his face.

10. Use a damp finger to pick up some red sanding sugar and very gently touch it to his cheeks to create the blushing effect.

11. Enjoy your adorable Santa!

CARDINAL CUPCAKES

MAKES 18 CUPCAKES

Cardinals look so beautiful against sparkling snow, and you'll love these even more in your tummy!

Cupcake Batter:
2 cups all-purpose flour
2 cups sugar
¾ cup cocoa powder
2 teaspoons baking powder
1½ teaspoons baking soda
1 teaspoon salt
1 cup milk
½ cup vegetable oil
2 large eggs
2 teaspoons vanilla extract
1 cup boiling water

Buttercream:
2 cups unsalted butter, room temperature
2 teaspoons vanilla extract
4 cups confectioners' sugar
Green and black food coloring
Red sprinkles, for the berries

Cardinals:
1¼ cups white chocolate, melted
2 cups melted red chocolate (or candy melts)
2 tablespoons melted dark chocolate
1 tablespoon melted white chocolate
9 yellow chocolate chip sprinkles

Cupcake Filling:
¾ cup white chocolate, melted
3 tablespoons whipping cream, hot
Dash of peppermint extract
¼ cup crushed candy canes

Bake the Cupcakes:
1. Preheat the oven to 350°F. Line two cupcake pans. You will need to bake 24 cupcakes to make 18 finished cupcakes with cardinals.

2. Place the flour, sugar, cocoa powder, baking powder, baking soda, and salt in a large bowl and mix together.

3. Add the milk, vegetable oil, eggs, and vanilla extract and mix with an electric mixer until combined.

4. Slowly add the boiling water and mix until well combined.

5. Divide the batter evenly between the pans and bake for 20 to 25 minutes, until a skewer inserted into the centers comes out clean. Cool completely.

Make the Buttercream:
1. Beat the butter with an electric mixer until pale and fluffy. Add the vanilla extract and milk and mix well. Add the confectioners' sugar 1 cup at a time, beating with each addition.

2. Dye the buttercream green.

3. Place the buttercream into a piping bag fitted with a medium-sized open star piping tip.

Make the Cardinals:
1. Crumble the ugliest 6 cupcakes into a bowl until they resemble a fine crumb. You can use an electric mixer, if desired.

(Continued on page 47)

2. Add the melted white chocolate and mix until fully combined. Divide the mixture into 18 pieces and roll them into balls.

3. Place on a plate lined with parchment paper or plastic wrap and chill in the fridge for 20 minutes.

4. Shape the balls into birds and chill in the fridge again for about 20 minutes.

5. Dip the birds into the melted red chocolate, return to the lined plate, and chill in the fridge while you decorate the cupcakes.

Make the Cupcake Filling:
1. Combine the white chocolate, cream, and peppermint extract in a bowl. Add the candy canes and fold to combine.

2. Spoon it into a piping bag and snip off the end to create a medium/large opening. It should be wide enough for the candy canes to pass through.

Decorate the Cupcakes:
1. Use a large piping tip or a knife to carve out the middles of the cupcakes. Pipe the ganache into the holes.

2. Using the green buttercream, pipe three rings of dollops onto each cupcake. One ring with the dollops pointing inward, one ring pointing outward, and one pointing upward. This will create the illusion of a natural wreath.

3. Sprinkle red sprinkles onto the wreath as berries.

4. Place the cardinals in the middle of the wreaths. Finish decorating the cardinals by creating their faces and eyes with the dark chocolate and white chocolate and their beaks with the yellow candy-coated chocolate chips. Enjoy!

FROZEN POND CUPCAKES

If you love cold weather, these cupcakes are for you! Not only do they have the cutest, most wintery scene on top, but they're also filled with blueberry jam and marshmallow fluff!

Pond and Ice Shards:
1¼ cups granulated sugar
½ cup water
½ cup light corn syrup
Blue food coloring
¼ teaspoon marshmallow flavoring
(optional, but delicious)

Cupcake Base:
½ cup unsalted butter, room temperature
1 cup granulated sugar
1½ teaspoon vanilla extract
3 large eggs, room temperature
1½ cups all-purpose flour
½ teaspoon baking soda
½ teaspoon salt
¾ cup sour cream
½ cup blueberry jam
Blue food coloring

Buttercream:
2 cups unsalted butter, room temperature
1 teaspoon vanilla extract
1 teaspoon peppermint extract
5 cups confectioners' sugar

Penguins:
¾ cup black fondant
¼ cup white fondant
Orange food coloring
Blue sprinkles
½ cup marshmallow fluff

½ cup blueberry jam
¼ cup silver sanding sugar
½ cup blue sanding sugar

Make the Pond and Ice Shards:

Note: This can be done a couple days in advance.

1. Place a 12-cavity silicone lollipop mold as well as a silicone baking mat next to your work surface. You'll need these as soon as the sugar is made.

2. Combine the sugar, water, and corn syrup in a deep pot over medium heat. Increase the heat to high and attach a candy thermometer to the pot. When the temperature reaches 300°F, add a tiny drop of blue food coloring and mix until fully combined. Bring the heat up to 310°F, then remove from the heat and stir with a rubber spatula until it stops bubbling.

3. Pour the candy into the silicone mold, creating 12 candy disks. Pour the remaining candy onto the silicone mat to create one sheet of candy. Allow to cool at room temperature, until hardened, about 1 to 2 hours. If making these in advance, store them as is, at room temperature, until needed.

Bake the Cupcakes:
1. Line a cupcake pan with cupcake liners and preheat the oven to 350°F.

(Continued on page 50)

2. Beat the butter and sugar with an electric mixer until pale and smooth. Add the vanilla extract and eggs one at a time, mixing with each addition.

3. In a separate bowl, combine the flour, baking soda, and salt. Add this to the batter in two phases, alternating with the sour cream. Then add the blueberry jam and a couple drops of blue food coloring and mix until combined.

4. Pour the batter into the cupcake pan and bake for 20 to 30 minutes, or until a skewer inserted into the center of the cupcakes comes out clean. Cool completely.

Make the Buttercream:
1. Place the butter in a large bowl and beat with an electric mixer until pale and fluffy. Add the vanilla and peppermint extract and mix to combine.

2. Add the confectioners' sugar 1 cup at a time, mixing with each addition. Then beat for another 3 minutes, until light and fluffy.

Make the Penguins:
1. Use the black fondant to create as many penguins as you like! Start by making round balls but be sure to save some black fondant for the wings. To make the wings, make 2 tiny ovals of black fondant and press them onto the sides of a ball.

2. To make the tummies, roll an even smaller ball of white fondant and flatten it between your fingers. Press it onto the tummy of the penguin.

3. Once you've made all the tummies, dye the remaining white fondant orange with orange food coloring. Roll a tiny oval for the beak and two more tiny ovals for the feet. Press them into the underside of the penguins, so that they stick out the front.

4. Use a skewer or tweezer to poke two holes for the eyes. Stick a blue sprinkle into each hole.

5. Set the penguins aside on a plate lined with plastic wrap. The plastic wrap will prevent them from sticking to the plate!

Assembly:
1. Use a small spoon or the wide end of a piping tip to carve a hole into the center of each cupcake. Fill each hole with a dollop of blueberry jam and marshmallow fluff.

2. Place a dollop of buttercream on top and spread to cover the surface of the cupcake. Don't worry if the edges are rough. Place a candy "pond" in the center of each cupcake.

3. Pour the blue and silver sanding sugar into a bowl. Roll the sides and top of the cupcake in the sugar.

4. Carefully break the large sheet of blue candy into shards. Stick these shards around the ponds.

5. Place the remaining white buttercream into a piping bag fitted with a small, star-shaped piping tip. Pipe a border around the ponds.

6. Stick the penguins onto the buttercream border and enjoy!

Snowflake Cupcakes

Clean, beautiful, and minimalistic! This technique of smoothing the buttercream to a flat surface is also a great canvas for writing buttercream messages. Create a few snowflake cupcakes, then throw a "Happy Holidays" message cupcake into the mix!

Cupcake Base:
½ cup unsalted butter, room temperature
1 cup granulated sugar
1½ teaspoon vanilla extract
1½ teaspoon peppermint extract
3 large eggs, room temperature
1½ cups all-purpose flour
½ teaspoon baking soda
½ teaspoon salt
¾ cup sour cream
1 cup white chocolate, melted
Blue food coloring

Buttercream:
2 cups unsalted butter, room temperature
1 teaspoon vanilla extract
1 teaspoon peppermint extract
5 cups confectioners' sugar
1 cup blue sanding sugar

Bake the Cupcakes:

1. Line a cupcake pan with cupcake liners and preheat the oven to 350°F.

2. Beat the butter and sugar with an electric mixer until pale and smooth. Add the vanilla extract, peppermint extract, and eggs one at a time, mixing with each addition.

3. In a separate bowl, combine the flour, baking soda, and salt. Add this to the batter in two phases, alternating with the sour cream. Then add the melted white chocolate and a couple drops of blue food coloring and mix until combined.

4. Pour the batter into the cupcake pan and bake for 20 to 25 minutes, or until a skewer inserted into the center of the cupcakes comes out clean. Cool completely.

Make the Buttercream:

1. Place the butter in a large bowl and beat with an electric mixer until pale and fluffy. Add the vanilla peppermint extracts and mix to combine.

2. Add the confectioners' sugar 1 cup at a time, mixing with each addition. Then beat for another 3 minutes, until light and fluffy.

(Continued on page 52)

Assembly:

1. Use a serrated knife to cut about ¼ inch off the tops of the cupcakes. These scraps can be eaten or saved for cake pops!

2. Place a generous dollop of buttercream on top of each cupcake. Spread it to the very edge of the cupcake and create a completely flat surface. Then run your knife around the edge of the cupcake so that you've created a flat edge of buttercream on the sides of the cupcake.

3. Pour the blue sanding sugar into a bowl and carefully roll just the sides of the cupcake into the sugar.

4. Place the cupcakes in the fridge for 15 minutes for the buttercream to stiffen.

5. Take a straw and, holding it at an angle, carve a snowflake shape into the buttercream. You may need to wipe down the straw between uses. Then enjoy!

ELF HAT CUPCAKES

These elf hat cupcakes are coming in with a citrusy kick with the help of lemon and lime zest! The hat portion is made from a cake pop base, so you have delicious, buttery goodness the entire way through the cupcake!

Cupcake Base:
½ cup unsalted butter, room temperature
1 cup granulated sugar
Zest from 2 lemons
Zest from 1 lime
1½ teaspoons vanilla extract
3 large eggs, room temperature
1½ cups all-purpose flour
½ teaspoon baking soda
½ teaspoon salt
¾ cup sour cream

Glaze:
Juice from 1 lemon
Juice from 1 lime
1 tablespoon granulated sugar
2 cups green melting wafers, melted

Buttercream:
1 cup unsalted butter, room temperature
1 teaspoon vanilla extract
2½ cups confectioners' sugar
Red food coloring
Edible glitter, for sprinkling

Bake the Cupcakes and Make the Glaze:

1. Line a cupcake pan with cupcake liners and preheat the oven to 350°F.

2. Beat the butter and sugar with an electric mixer until pale and smooth. Add the lemon and lime zest, vanilla extract, and eggs one at a time, mixing with each addition.

3. In a separate bowl, combine the flour, baking soda, and salt. Add this to the batter in two phases, alternating with the sour cream.

4. Pour the batter into the cupcake pan and bake for 20 to 25 minutes, or until a skewer inserted into the center of the cupcakes comes out clean.

5. Whisk together the ingredients for the glaze in a small bowl and brush onto the cupcakes while they're still warm. Then allow them to cool completely.

Assembly:

1. Crumble 4 of the cupcakes into a bowl. Use steps 1 to 2 from the Snowball Cake Pops recipe (page 3) to create a cake pop base.

2. Divide the cake pop mixture into 8 and use it to build the elf hats directly on top of the bare cupcakes.

3. Place the cupcakes in the fridge for 15 minutes for the hats to stiffen.

(Continued on page 56)

4. Pour the green candy wafers into a narrow bowl and dunk the cupcakes into it, making sure that the elf hats are fully coated.

5. Return the cupcakes to the fridge while you make the buttercream.

Make the Buttercream:

1. Place the butter in a large bowl and beat with an electric mixer until pale and fluffy. Add the vanilla extract and mix to combine.

2. Add the confectioners' sugar 1 cup at a time, mixing with each addition. Then beat for another 3 minutes, until light and fluffy.

3. Dye two thirds of the buttercream red with red food coloring. Place half of the red buttercream into a piping bag fitted with a medium-sized star-shaped piping tip. Place the other half into a piping bag fitted with a small, round piping tip.

4. Place the white buttercream into a piping bag fitted with small, star-shaped piping tip.

Decorate:

1. Using the red buttercream with the star-shaped tip, pipe a trim around the edge of the elf hat. Use the other red buttercream to pipe your desired pattern and swirls onto the hats.

2. Use the white buttercream to pipe dollops between the red trim, as well as a pompom on the tip of the hat. Sprinkle some edible glitter on top of the pompom. Enjoy!

COOKIES

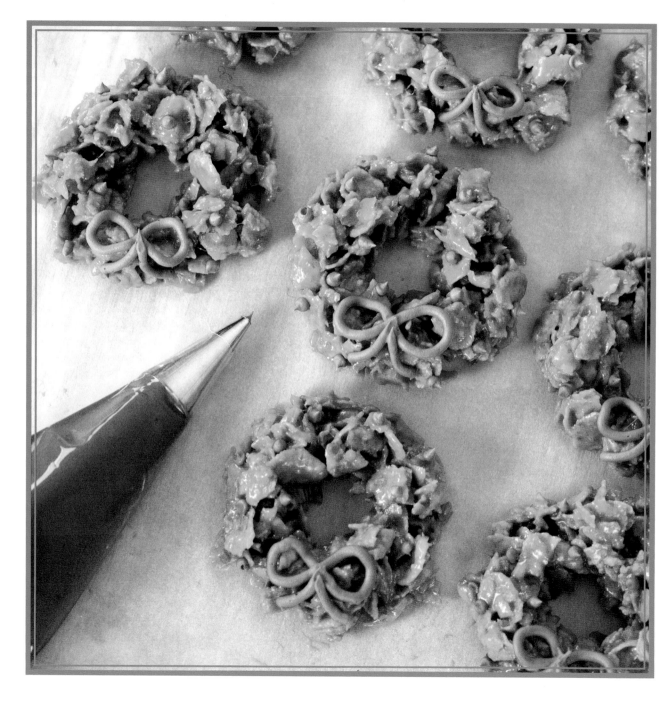

CORNFLAKE WREATH COOKIES

MAKES 12 COOKIES

These cute cookies are perfect if you don't have access to an oven or are just tired of rolling out endless balls of cookie dough!

½ cup unsalted butter

3 cups mini marshmallows

1 teaspoon vanilla extract

Pinch of salt

Green food coloring

3 cups cornflakes

Cooking spray

½ batch Classic Royal Icing, dyed red (page 93)

1. Place the butter in a large, microwave-safe bowl. Heat it for 30-second intervals, until melted.

2. Add the mini marshmallows, mix to fully coat them in butter, then return the bowl to the microwave and heat it for 30-second intervals until the marshmallows have fully melted.

3. Add the vanilla extract, salt, and a couple drops of green food coloring and mix well.

4. Add the cornflakes and mix vigorously until the cornflakes are evenly coated. Allow the mixture to cool slightly until it can be easily handled.

5. Line a baking sheet with parchment paper. Lightly coat your hands with cooking spray. Take about 2 tablespoons of cornflakes and shape them into a ring shape on the baking sheet. Repeat with the remaining cornflakes and allow the wreaths to fully cool and stiffen, 2 to 3 hours or overnight.

6. Place the Classic Royal Icing in a piping bag fitted with a small, round piping tip. Pipe a bow at the base of each wreath and berries all over the wreath. Allow the icing to harden, about 1 hour, then enjoy!

SNICKERDOODLES

MAKES APPROXIMATELY 2 DOZEN (1-INCH) COOKIES

A simple holiday cookie that I absolutely love having with my tea or coffee in the morning. They're not too sweet, but sweet enough to feel like I'm enjoying the holidays at every moment of the day!

Cookie Dough:
½ cup unsalted butter, room temperature
½ cup shortening
1½ cups white sugar
2 large eggs
2 teaspoons vanilla extract
2¾ cups all-purpose flour
2 teaspoons cream of tartar
1 teaspoon baking soda
½ teaspoon salt

Topping:
2 tablespoons white sugar
2 teaspoons ground cinnamon

1. Preheat the oven to 440°F.

2. First, make the cookie dough. Place the butter, shortening, sugar, eggs, and vanilla in a bowl and beat with an electric mixer until smooth. Add the flour, cream of tartar, baking soda, and salt. Mix until just combined.

3. Shape the dough into balls. Set aside.

4. Combine the sugar and cinnamon for the topping. Roll the balls in the topping mixture. Place the cookies on a baking sheet lined with parchment paper, spacing them about 1 to 2 inches apart.

5. Bake for 8 minutes, until set but not too firm. Cool completely and enjoy!

Mistletoe Balls

I love these. I love these so much. Not only do they taste far better than the store-bought equivalent, but these are perfect for packing into lunch boxes or snacking on while watching holiday movies.

¼ cup unsalted butter

5 cups mini marshmallows

1 teaspoon vanilla extract

Green food coloring

4 cups crispy rice cereal

¼ cup marshmallow bits

3 rolls pink Fruit by the Foot

1. Melt the butter in a pot over low heat. Add the mini marshmallows and mix until fully melted. Remove from the heat and add the vanilla extract and green food coloring. Add the cereal and mix well.

2. Allow the mixture to cool until it is easily handled. Spray your hands with cooking spray and shape the mixture into 12 balls.

3. Stick marshmallow bits in clusters of 3 all over the balls, to look like mistletoe berries.

4. To create the bows, take a 3-inch-long piece of Fruit by the Foot and create a loop shape. Wrap another piece around the center, pinching the loop together to create a bow! Use two more strips as the bow's "tails" and stick these on top of the balls. The marshmallow coating should be sticky enough for the bows to stick.

GINGERBREAD COOKIES FOR DOGS

MAKES 15-20 COOKIES

Include your pup in your holiday festivities! Ginger is actually great for dogs and can help reduce nausea, so if you're doing lots of traveling this season, make a couple cookies for your dog to enjoy during the car ride!

3 tablespoons olive oil
¼ cup + 2 tablespoons water
¼ cup molasses
1 teaspoon freshly grated ginger
2 teaspoons ground ginger
1½ cups all-purpose flour

1. Preheat over to 325°F.

2. Combine the olive oil, water, molasses, and fresh ginger with an electric mixer. Add the ground ginger and flour and mix until just combined.

3. Wrap the dough in plastic wrap and chill in the fridge for 1 hour.

4. Roll the dough out between 2 sheets of plastic wrap. Cut out cookies and place them on a baking sheet lined with parchment paper.

5. Bake the cookies for 20 minutes. Cool completely, then give to your pup and wrap some presents!

Edible Gold Coins

MAKES AS MANY AS YOU NEED!

I used to get a bag of chocolate gold coins in my stocking every year and I've loved creating this homemade version! Perfect for cookie exchanges or as a surprise treat at the holiday dinner table.

Chocolate sandwich cookies
Edible gold color spray

1. Place the cookies on a baking sheet lined with parchment paper. Spray with the gold color spray until evenly coated.

2. Flip over and repeat on the opposite side.

3. Allow the cookies to dry, about 2 hours, then enjoy!

Santa's Cookies

MAKES 44 COOKIES

Santa has a long journey to make, so we can't skimp on cookie ingredients! We're adding everything—almost including the kitchen sink—into these cookies, creating salty, sweet, chocolaty goodness! I'm certain that these will fuel Santa the rest of his way!

2¼ cups all-purpose flour

½ teaspoon baking soda

1 cup unsalted butter, room temperature

½ cup granulated sugar

1 cup brown sugar

1 teaspoons salt

2 teaspoons vanilla extract

2 large eggs

1 cup red and green candy-coated chocolates

½ cup chocolate chips

½ cup crushed pretzels

½ cup crushed potato chips

1. Preheat the oven to 350°F.

2. Combine the flour and baking soda in a bowl.

3. In a separate bowl, beat the butter, granulated sugar, brown sugar, and salt with an electric mixer until smooth and creamy. Add the vanilla extract and eggs and beat until combined. Add the flour mixture and mix until just combined.

4. Add the red and green chocolate, chocolate chips, pretzels, and potato chips and mix with a spoon until evenly incorporated.

5. Place 2 tablespoons-sized balls of dough on a baking sheet lined with parchment paper. Chill the cookies in the fridge for 20 minutes, then bake for 10 to 13 minutes, until the edges are just starting to brown.

6. Cool for a few minutes and enjoy!

Classic Gingerbread Cookies

Such a holiday classic! Decorate with royal icing or leave plain—these are delicious in every way!

Cookie Base:
2 cups all-purpose flour
2 teaspoons ground ginger
1 teaspoon ground cinnamon
½ teaspoon ground nutmeg
¼ teaspoon ground cloves
¼ teaspoon baking soda
¼ teaspoon salt
½ cup unsalted butter, room temperature
⅓ cup brown sugar
⅓ cup molasses
1 large egg

Royal Icing:
½ pound (2 cups) confectioners' sugar
2½ tablespoons meringue powder
Scant ¼ cup water

Bake the Cookies:

1. Preheat the oven to 350°F.

2. Combine the flour, ginger, cinnamon, nutmeg, cloves, baking soda, and salt. Set aside.

3. In a separate bowl, beat the butter and brown sugar with an electric mixer until light and fluffy. Add the molasses and egg and mix well.

4. Add the dry ingredients and mix until just combined.

5. Shape the dough into a ball and wrap in plastic wrap. Chill in the fridge for 1 hour or overnight.

6. Flour your work surface and roll the dough out until it is ⅛- to ¼-inch thick. Cut out your desired shapes, then place them on a baking sheet lined with parchment paper.

7. Bake for 10 minutes, until the edges are just starting to brown. Cool completely.

Make the Royal Icing:

1. Place the confectioners' sugar, meringue powder, and water into a bowl. Beat with an electric mixer on high for 7 minutes, until stiff peaks form. If it feels too thick, you can add an extra 1 to 2 tablespoons water but do so very gradually.

2. Place the icing into a piping bag fitted with a #2 small, round piping tip. Pipe your designs onto the cookies.

3. Allow the icing to harden, about 1 hour. Then enjoy!

Red Velvet Gingerbread Cookies

Red velvet is delicious and absolutely needs to take over the gingerbread world! These cookies are delicious and such a fun twist at any cookie exchange. For an extra-special touch, add some cream cheese flavoring to the Classic Royal Icing!

2 cups all-purpose flour
2 tablespoons cocoa powder
3 teaspoons Gingerbread Spice Mix
  (page 93)
¼ teaspoon baking soda
¼ teaspoon salt
½ cup unsalted butter, room temperature
⅓ cup brown sugar
⅓ cup molasses
1 large egg
Red gel food coloring
½ teaspoon cheesecake flavoring
1 batch Classic Royal Icing (page 93)

Bake the Cookies:

1. Preheat the oven to 350°F.

2. Combine the flour, cocoa powder, Gingerbread Spice Mix, baking soda, and salt. Set aside.

3. In a separate bowl, beat the butter and brown sugar with an electric mixer until light and fluffy. Add the molasses, egg, and food coloring and mix well.

4. Add the dry ingredients and mix until just combined.

5. Shape the dough into a ball and wrap in plastic wrap. Chill in the freezer for 1 hour.

6. Place the dough between two floured sheets of parchment paper and roll the dough out until it is ⅛- to ¼-inch thick. This dough is a little softer than classic gingerbread, so don't hesitate to return it to the freezer to chill when needed.

7. Cut out your desired shapes, then place them on a baking sheet lined with parchment paper. Place the baking sheet into the freezer and freeze for 20 minutes, until very firm.

8. Bake for 12 minutes, until the edges are just starting to brown. Cool completely.

Decorate:

1. Add the cheesecake flavoring to the Classic Royal Icing for an extra "red velvet" touch!

2. Place the icing into a piping bag fitted with a small, round piping tip. Pipe your designs onto the cookies.

3. Allow the icing to harden, about 1 hour. Then enjoy!

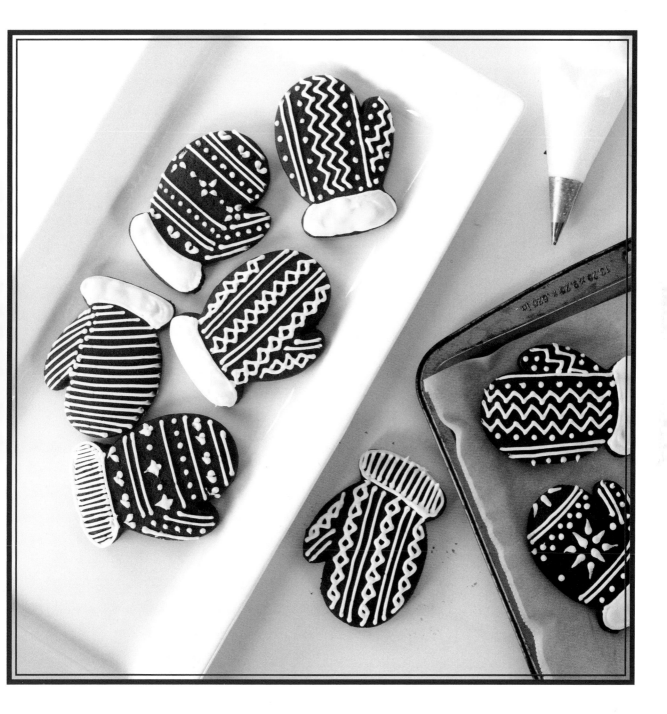

Candy Cane Eclairs, page 84

OTHER TREATS

Mini Gingerbread Doughnuts

MAKES APPROXIMATELY 2 DOZEN MINI DOUGHNUTS

These little doughnuts are a fun and simple weeknight treat and only need a dusting of confectioners' sugar for decoration. Whip up a batch and snuggle under a blanket to watch your favorite holiday movie.

2 cups all-purpose flour

1½ cups granulated sugar

2 teaspoons baking powder

3 teaspoons Gingerbread Spice Mix (page 93)

½ teaspoon salt

1 large egg, room temperature

1¼ cups milk, room temperature

2 tablespoons unsalted butter, melted

2 teaspoons vanilla extract

Cooking spray

Confectioners' sugar, for dusting

1. Preheat the oven to 350°F.

2. Place the flour, sugar, baking powder, Gingerbread Spice Mix, and salt in a large bowl, and mix together.

3. In a separate bowl, combine the egg, milk, melted butter, and vanilla extract. Then add this to the dry mixture and mix together. Place the batter into a piping bag and snip off the end—this will make it so much easier to fill the pan!

4. Grease a mini doughnut pan with cooking spray. Pipe the batter into the doughnut pan and bake for 6 to 8 minutes, or until a skewer inserted into the doughnuts comes out clean. Place the doughnuts on a cooling rack to cool.

5. Dust on some confectioners' sugar, and you're done!

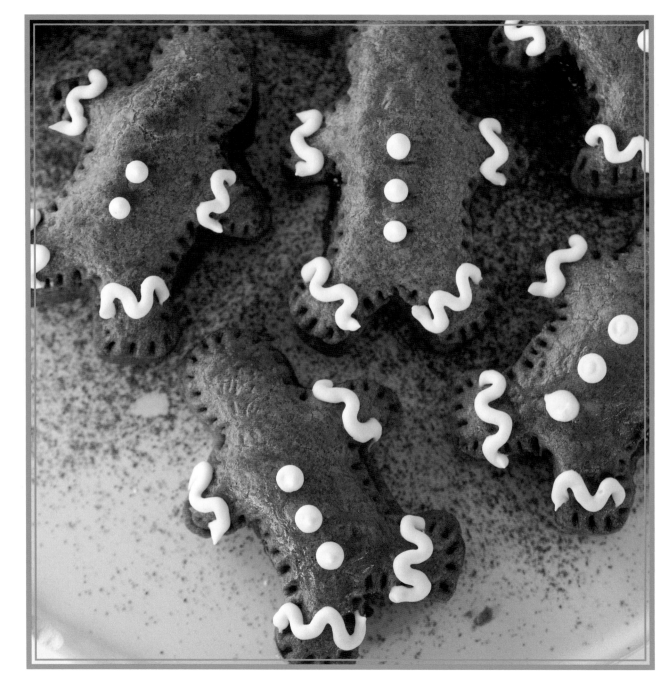

Mini Gingerbread Man Toaster Pastries

MAKES 14

These cute little gingerbread men are filled with apricot jam, which pairs so deliciously well with the gingerbread piecrust!

Pie Dough:

2½ cups all-purpose flour
1 teaspoon Gingerbread Spice Mix
    (page 93)
1 teaspoon salt
1 teaspoon sugar
1 cup cold unsalted butter, cut into cubes
¼–½ cup cold water
Brown food coloring
1 large egg, beaten
½ cup apricot jam
½ batch Classic Royal Icing (page 93)

Make the Dough:

1. Mix the flour, Gingerbread Spice Mix, salt, and sugar in a food processor. Add the butter and pulse until it turns into a crumbly/mealy texture.

2. Add a couple drops of brown food coloring to the water, then pour it into the food processor. Pulse until the dough sticks together when squished.

3. Shape the dough into a ball and wrap in plastic wrap. Place in the refrigerator for 1 hour, until firm.

Assembly:

1. Preheat the oven to 400°F and line a baking sheet with parchment paper.

2. Roll the dough out on a floured surface to ¼-inch thick. Use a 3-inch gingerbread man cookie cutter to cut out 28 gingerbread men.

3. Place 14 of the gingerbread men onto the baking sheet. Gently press into the center of the gingerbread man to create an indent for the filling.

4. Spoon a dollop of apricot jam into each indent. Wet your finger and wet the edges of the gingerbread men and place the other 14 gingerbread men on top, gently pressing to seal them together.

5. Use the edge of a fork to seal edges together and make the little notches. Then brush the surface of the gingerbread men with the beaten egg.

6. Chill them in the fridge for about 10 minutes, then bake for 15 minutes or until golden. Cool completely.

7. To decorate, place the Classic Royal Icing into a piping bag fitted with a small, round piping tip. Pipe squiggles on the hands and feet, as well as buttons down the middle. Enjoy!

Gnome Cookie Cups

MAKES 24

For such cute little gnomes, they are perfectly balanced in flavor! The tartness of the fresh strawberry cuts through the sweetness of the cookie base and their cream cheese beards add a delicious tang that makes these seriously addictive! Pop them into your lunch or simply pop one into your mouth every time you enter the kitchen!

Cookie Cups:
Cooking spray
2¼ cups all-purpose flour
½ teaspoon baking soda
1 cup unsalted butter, room temperature
½ cup granulated sugar
1 cup brown sugar
1 teaspoon salt
2 teaspoons vanilla extract
2 large eggs
24 mini peanut butter cups

Gnome Beards:
8 ounces cream cheese, room temperature
½ cup unsalted butter, room temperature
1 teaspoon vanilla extract
3 cups confectioners' sugar
24 strawberries, greens removed
24 candy-coated chocolates

Bake the Cups:
1. Preheat the oven to 350°F. Spray two mini muffin pans generously with cooking spray.

2. Combine the flour and baking soda in a bowl.

3. In a separate bowl, beat the butter, granulated sugar, brown sugar, and salt with an electric mixer until smooth and creamy. Add the vanilla extract and eggs and beat until combined. Add the flour mixture and mix until just combined.

4. Roll 2 tablespoons of dough into balls and place one into each cavity of the muffin pan. Bake for 20 minutes, until the edges are just starting to brown.

5. As soon as they come out of the oven, press a mini peanut butter cup into the center of each cookie cup. Use a knife or spoon to help you push it downward because the cookie will be hot!

6. Allow the cookies to cool almost completely in the pan, then gently unmold and allow them to finish cooling on a rack.

Make the Beards:
1. Place the cream cheese and butter in a bowl and beat with an electric mixer until smooth. Add the vanilla extract and mix until combined.

2. Add the confectioners' sugar 1 cup at a time, beating with each addition. Then beat for an additional 3 minutes, until light and fluffy.

Assembly:
1. Place a dollop of frosting on top of a cookie cup and place a strawberry on top.

2. Spread some more frosting onto the front of the cookie cup to create the beard and stick a chocolate onto the beard as the gnome's nose.

3. Enjoy your sweet little gnomes!

GINGERBREAD CHEESECAKE SWIRL BROWNIES

MAKES 16 BROWNIES

The best of both worlds—cheesecake AND gingerbread, swirled together in chocolaty goodness! If you're looking to indulge, this is the dessert to make!

Brownie Batter:
Cooking spray
12 ounces bittersweet chocolate
1 cup unsalted butter
3 cups granulated sugar
6 large eggs
½ cup cocoa powder
1 tablespoon instant coffee or espresso powder
1 teaspoon Gingerbread Spice Mix (page 93)
Pinch of salt
1¼ cup all-purpose flour

Cheesecake Layer:
8 ounces cream cheese, room temperature
⅓ cup granulated sugar
1 large egg yolk
1½ teaspoon vanilla extract
2 teaspoons Gingerbread Spice Mix (page 93)
2 tablespoons mini chocolate chips
2 tablespoons white chocolate chips

1. Preheat the oven to 350°F. Grease a square 9 × 9–inch cake pan with cooking spray and line with parchment paper, ensuring that excess parchment paper is hanging off of both sides.

2. Place the bittersweet chocolate and butter in a heatproof bowl over a pot of simmering water. Stir until fully melted, then remove from the heat.

3. Gradually whisk in the sugar and add the eggs one at a time, mixing after each addition. Add the cocoa powder, instant coffee or espresso powder, Gingerbread Spice Mix, and the pinch of salt.

4. Gently fold the flour into the mixture with a rubber spatula. Set aside.

5. Now, make the cheesecake layer. Place the cream cheese and granulated sugar in a bowl and beat with an electric mixer until smooth. Add the egg yolk, vanilla extract, and Gingerbread Spice Mix and mix until fully incorporated.

6. Pour half of the brownie mixture into the pan and smooth the surface. Pour half of the cheesecake mixture on top. Pour the remaining brownie mixture on top and spread to the edges of the pan. Place dollops of the remaining cheesecake mixture onto the surface and swirl it into the brownie batter. Sprinkle the chocolate chips on top.

7. Bake for 60 to 80 minutes or until fully cooked. Keep an eye on the brownies—if you feel like the cheesecake layer is browning too much, loosely cover the pan with a sheet of aluminum foil.

8. Place the pan on a wire rack and allow the brownies to cool completely while still in the pan. Cut into squares and enjoy!

Candy Cane Eclairs

These eclairs are light and crispy and are filled with my fail-safe chocolate peppermint pastry cream. I actually used to be super intimidated by eclairs and cream puffs, but I promise that this recipe works every single time, and you'll have success, even if you're a beginner baker!

Pastry Cream:
½ cup sugar
¼ cup cornstarch
Pinch of salt
2 cups milk
4 large egg yolks
1 tablespoon cocoa powder
1½ teaspoon vanilla extract
1 teaspoon peppermint extract
2 tablespoons unsalted butter, cold

Choux Pastry:
1 cup water
½ cup unsalted butter, cold and cut into
   cubes
1 teaspoon sugar
½ teaspoon salt
1 cup all-purpose flour
4 large eggs

Glaze:
1 cup confectioners' sugar
2 tablespoons whipping cream
Red food coloring
Crushed candy canes

Make the Pastry Cream:

1. Combine the sugar, cornstarch, and salt in a pot. Add the milk, egg yolks, and cocoa powder and whisk together. Set to medium heat and whisk constantly until it comes to a boil. Once it thickens, remove from the heat and add the vanilla and peppermint extracts and butter.

2. Strain through a sieve and cover with plastic wrap, pressing it directly on the surface. Refrigerate until chilled. If the pastry cream becomes lumpy, pulse in a food processor a couple times. Transfer to a piping bag fitted with a round tip.

Make the Eclairs:

1. Preheat the oven to 375°F and line a baking sheet with parchment paper.

2. In a large pot, combine the water, butter, sugar, and salt. Set to high heat and bring to a boil. Stir in the flour with a wooden spoon mix until a film forms on the bottom of the pan. Transfer the dough to a bowl and cool for 3 to 4 minutes. Add the eggs one at a time, stirring vigorously and completely incorporating each egg after each addition.

3. Transfer the dough to a piping bag fitted with a large, round piping tip and pipe 5-inch eclairs onto the baking sheet. Wet your fingers and smooth any pointed peaks.

4. Bake them for 30 minutes, until golden. Cool on the pan for 10 minutes, then transfer to a wire rack and cool completely.

5. Poke holes in the base of the eclairs and fill with pastry cream.

Decorate:
1. Combine the confectioners' sugar and whipping cream in a bowl. Add a couple drops of red food coloring and very slightly swirl with a knife. Swirl it less than you want to, as it will continue to swirl as you use it.

2. Dip the tops of the eclairs into the glaze. Allow the glaze to set for about 10 minutes, then sprinkle crushed candy canes on top. Enjoy! These eclairs are best eaten the day they are filled.

Frozen Icy Doughnuts

These delicate, tender doughnuts are baked, not fried, and look as if an ice queen glazed them with an icy blizzard! These doughnuts also bake in just 7 minutes, making them a perfect treat when you don't have a lot of time on your hands.

Doughnut Batter:
Cooking spray
1 cup all-purpose flour
1 teaspoon baking powder
¼ teaspoon salt
3 tablespoons unsalted butter, melted
¼ cup sugar
2 tablespoons honey
1 large egg
¼ teaspoon vanilla extract
Blue food coloring
⅓ cup + 1 tablespoon buttermilk

Glaze:
3 tablespoons whipping cream
1 cup confectioners' sugar
Blue food coloring
Blue sanding sugar

Bake the Doughnuts:

1. Preheat the oven to 400°F. Spray a doughnut pan with cooking spray.

2. Whisk together the flour, baking powder, and salt in a small bowl and set aside. In a large bowl, combine the butter, sugar, honey, egg, vanilla, and blue food coloring. Add the buttermilk and mix until combined. Add the dry ingredients and mix until just combined—make sure not to overmix.

3. Spoon the batter into a piping bag. Pipe the batter into the doughnut pan and bake at 7 minutes. Cool for 1 minute in the pan, then flip the pan over to remove the doughnuts and cool completely on a wire rack.

Decorate:

1. Whisk together the whipping cream and the confectioners' sugar and until fully combined. Add a drop of blue food coloring and mix well.

2. Dunk each doughnut into the glaze and return to the wire rack.

3. Dunk the doughnut again into the blue sanding sugar. Admire how sparkly your doughnuts have become and enjoy!

HOT CHOCOLATE PIE

Chocolate lovers, this one is for you! This pie is insanely rich with its chocolate cookie crust and milk chocolate custard filling. If you'd like to add a festive touch, add a dash of peppermint extract to the whipped cream topping and a sprinkle of crushed candy canes on top.

Piecrust:
24 chocolate sandwich cookies
5 tablespoons unsalted butter, melted

Filling:
1 cup granulated sugar
½ cup cornstarch
Pinch of salt
4 cups milk
8 large egg yolks
2 tablespoons cocoa powder
3 teaspoons vanilla extract
2 tablespoons unsalted butter, cold and cut into cubes
8 ounces milk chocolate, chopped

Topping:
1 cup whipping cream, cold
3 tablespoons confectioners' sugar
1 teaspoon vanilla extract
¼ cup milk chocolate, finely chopped

Make the Piecrust:
1. Preheat the oven to 350°F.

2. Place the sandwich cookies, filling included, into a food processor and pulse until it resembles a fine crumb. Add the melted butter and pulse until well combined.

3. Press the crust into an 11-inch fluted pie pan with a removable bottom. Bake for 10 to 12 minutes, until dark and firm. Cool completely.

Make the Filling:
1. Combine the sugar, cornstarch, and salt in a pot. Add the milk, egg yolks, and cocoa powder and whisk together. Set to medium heat and whisk constantly until it comes to a boil. Once it thickens, remove from the heat and add the vanilla extract, butter, and milk chocolate.

2. Strain through a sieve and cover with plastic wrap, pressing it directly on the surface. Refrigerate until chilled. If the custard becomes lumpy, pulse in a food processor a couple times.

3. Pour the custard into the tart shell and chill in the fridge overnight.

Topping:
1. Place the whipping cream in a bowl and beat with an electric mixer until soft peaks form. Add the confectioners' sugar and vanilla extract and beat until stiff peaks form.

2. Dollop the cream on top of the tart. Sprinkle the chopped milk chocolate on top and serve!

Santa Hat Cream Puffs

This recipe uses oil-based food coloring to dye the chocolate coating. This is because chocolate will seize if water is added, and regular liquid and gel food coloring contains water! If you don't have access to oil-based food coloring, you can simply replace the white chocolate with red candy wafers.

Choux Pastry:
1 cup water
½ cup unsalted butter, cold and cut into cubes
1 teaspoon sugar
½ teaspoon salt
1 cup all-purpose flour
4 large eggs
1 cup melted white chocolate
Red oil-based food coloring

Filling:
1 cup whipping cream, cold
2 tablespoons confectioners' sugar
1 teaspoon vanilla extract

Make the Cream Puffs:

1. Preheat the oven to 375°F and line a baking sheet with parchment paper.

2. In a large pot, combine the water, butter, sugar, and salt. Set to high heat and bring to a boil. Stir in the flour with a wooden spoon and mix until a film forms on the bottom of the pan. Transfer the dough to a bowl and cool for 3 to 4 minutes. Add the eggs one at a time, stirring vigorously and completely incorporating each egg after each addition.

3. Transfer the dough to a piping bag fitted with a large, round piping tip and pipe 2-inch rounds onto the baking sheet. Wet your fingers and smooth any pointed peaks.

4. Bake them for 30 minutes, until golden. Cool on the pan for 10 minutes, then transfer to a wire rack and cool completely.

Assembly:

1. Use a serrated knife to cut the cream puffs in half.

2. Add a couple drops of oil-based food coloring to the melted white chocolate, dyeing it red.

3. Dip the tops of the cream puffs into the chocolate, place them on a tray, and pop them into the fridge for the chocolate to set.

Make the Filling:

1. Place the whipping cream, confectioners' sugar, and vanilla extract in a bowl. Beat with an electric mixer and beat until stiff peaks form.

2. Place the cream in a piping bag fitted with a medium-sized star-shaped piping tip.

Serve:

1. Right before serving, add the cream filling. Pipe a generous swirl of cream into the base of a cream puff, then place the top half back on top.

2. Pipe another dollop of cream on top as the pompom to the hat. Serve immediately and enjoy!

GINGERBREAD SPICE MIX

Turn everything in your kitchen into gingerbread! This spice mix is very fragrant and will definitely put you into a festive mood.

1 tablespoon + 1 teaspoon ground
   cinnamon
1 tablespoon ground ginger
1 tablespoon ground allspice
1½ teaspoon ground nutmeg
1½ teaspoon ground cloves

1. Place all the spices in a bowl and mix well.

2. To store, place it in an airtight jar alongside your other spices.

CLASSIC ROYAL ICING

MAKES ABOUT 4 CUPS

The perfect royal icing for gingerbread houses or cookies! This royal icing is thick enough to pipe and hold its shape, however if you'd like it to run more for flooding cookies, gradually add small amounts of water until your desired consistency is achieved.

¾ cup warm water
5 tablespoons meringue powder
1 teaspoon cream of tartar
8 cups confectioners' sugar
1 teaspoon vanilla extract or any desired
   flavoring (optional)
Food coloring (optional)

1. Pour the warm water into a large bowl. Add the meringue powder and whisk for a couple seconds, until frothy. Add the cream of tartar and whisk again.

2. Add the confectioners' sugar and, using an electric mixer, mix on low speed for 10 minutes.

3. At this point, if desired, add the vanilla extract and mix until well combined. Then add food coloring, if you like!

4. Be sure to cover the bowl with a damp dish towel or plastic wrap to prevent it from drying out.

Simple Syrup

Simple syrup can be used to sweeten drinks or brushed onto cakes for additional moisture! If you're feeling creative, you can flavor your syrup for an extra touch.

1 cup granulated sugar
1 cup water

1. Place the sugar and water in a small pot and stir until the sugar has dissolved.

2. Set the pot to medium heat and bring the syrup to a boil.

3. Once the syrup becomes clear, turn off the heat and you're done! It's really that simple!

Note: To flavor this syrup, once the syrup comes to a boil, add your desired spices or fruit, then reduce the heat to low and simmer, covered, for about 10 minutes. Remove the pot from the heat and allow the syrup to cool for about 1 hour. This will give enough time for the ingredients to infuse deliciously into the syrup. Then strain the syrup and enjoy! I recommend trying freshly sliced ginger, vanilla beans, pumpkin spice mix, or cinnamon sticks.

Homemade Vanilla Extract

This vanilla extract can be made in advance of your holiday baking or used as a beautiful Christmas gift for friends and family!

5–6 dried vanilla beans
1 cup 80-proof vodka (or bourbon, brandy, or rum—whichever you like!)

1. Slice the vanilla beans down the center with a sharp knife. You don't need to split them open, just make sure the knife pierces the skin.

2. Place the vanilla beans into a jar. If they are too tall for the jar, slice them in half lengthwise.

3. Fill the jar with vodka, making sure to fully submerge the beans. They will get a little slimy if not fully submerged.

4. Store in a cool, dry place for 8 weeks to 6 months, until the extract is at its optimal flavor. Shake the bottle about once a week.

5. The extract can be topped up with more vodka as you use it. Just make sure that the beans are always submerged. It should last several years!

Candy Cane Rocky Road Fudge, page 107

CANDY

PIGGY PEPPERMINT BARK

MAKES 16 (1-INCH) TRUFFLES

These little pigs are frozen from the chilly weather! White chocolate and peppermint is an absolutely delicious combination that I feel is nowhere near as popular as it should be!

2¼ cups white chocolate, melted
Pink oil-based food coloring
½ cup crispy rice cereal
¼ cup candy canes, crushed
White luster dust (optional)

1. Dye half of the white chocolate pink with the pink oil-based food coloring. Fill a pig-shaped silicone mold halfway with the pink chocolate. Sprinkle some cereal on top of the chocolate. Place the mold in the freezer for the chocolate to fully set, about 15 minutes.

2. Pour the white chocolate on top and sprinkle some crushed candy canes on the surface. Return the mold to the freezer for the chocolate to set for an additional 20 minutes.

3. Unmold the chocolates and dust the pigs' faces with white luster dust to give them a frosty look.

Note: Regular liquid or gel food coloring cannot be used to dye chocolate because it contains water, which will cause the chocolate to seize. That's why I used oil-based food coloring in this recipe, as oil can be added to chocolate without problem! It used to be tricky to find but now can be found online quite easily. If you can't get your hands on pink oil-based food coloring for this recipe, try substituting a couple teaspoons of dehydrated raspberry powder!

Homemade Holiday Sprinkles

The ultimate trick to custom holiday cake decorating! Create classic colors like red, green, and white or go wild with a sugarplum vibe (pink, purple, white, and gold) or a snowy mood (light blue, dark blue, white, and gray).

¾ cup warm water
5 tablespoons meringue powder
1 teaspoon cream of tartar
8 cups confectioners' sugar
Red and green gel food coloring

1. Pour the warm water into a large bowl. Add the meringue powder and whisk for a couple seconds, until frothy. Add the cream of tartar and whisk again.

2. Add the confectioners' sugar and, using an electric mixer, mix on low speed for 10 minutes.

3. Divide the mixture into 3 bowls. Using the food coloring, dye one bowl red, one bowl green, and leave the remaining bowl white.

4. Place the mixture into piping bags fitted with small, round piping tips. Line several baking sheets with parchment paper and pipe long, straight lines of every color over and over again. Fill up the baking sheets!

5. Allow the sprinkles to dry at room temperature for a full 24 hours.

6. Use your hands or a knife to break the long sprinkles into small pieces, then use in your baking or store in an airtight jar!

MELTING IGLOO DESSERT

MAKES 4

If you love white chocolate, you'll love this dessert! The prep work can be done in advance, so that when it's time to eat, you can enjoy the show of the igloo melting before your eyes! If you'd like to cut the sweetness a little, place some fresh raspberries alongside the vanilla ice cream underneath the igloo and use dark chocolate instead of white chocolate when making the ganache.

2¼ cups white chocolate, melted
¼ cup edible glitter
4 chocolate cupcake tops (from Reindeer
   Cupcakes, page 5)
¼ cup mini marshmallows

White Chocolate Ganache:
¾ cup white chocolate
¼ cup whipping cream
Pinch of salt
4 scoops vanilla ice cream
Confectioners' sugar, for dusting

Prep:

1. Coat the inside of four (3-inch-wide) dome-shaped silicone molds with white chocolate. Aim for the chocolate to be about 1 millimeter thick. Place the mold in the freezer for the chocolate to harden.

2. Place some more white chocolate in a piping bag fitted with a round tip and make a swirly pattern on four serving plates. Sprinkle with some edible glitter. Place a cupcake top in the center of each plate and dust with confectioners' sugar. Dip some mini marshmallows into water and then dip into the edible glitter. Arrange these around the plate to look like snowballs.

3. Remove the chocolate domes from the mold and place each dome on a square of parchment paper. Pipe some more melted white chocolate onto the igloos to look like little bricks. Return to the freezer to set.

4. Pipe the remaining white chocolate into a bear-shaped silicone mold, making 4 polar bears. Place the mold in the freezer for the chocolate to set.

Make the Ganache:

1. Finely chop the white chocolate and place it in a bowl.

(Continued on page 106)

2. Place the whipping cream in a microwave-safe bowl and heat for 30 second intervals until hot. Pour this on top of the chocolate, add the salt, and whisk until the chocolate has fully melted. Set aside.

Serve:

1. Place a scoop of vanilla ice cream on top of the cupcake top. Place an igloo on top. Dust some confectioners' sugar on top. Place a chocolate bear next to the igloo.

2. Place the plates at the table and have your guests sit down.

3. Very quickly, microwave the White Chocolate Ganache for about 30 seconds until it starts bubbling. Immediately pour it on top of the igloo to melt it and reveal the ice cream!

CANDY CANE ROCKY ROAD FUDGE

You absolutely need to try this out! The white chocolate is balanced with the freshness of the minty candy cane. The marshmallows add a pillowy softness that is countered by the texture of the nuts and candies. You will struggle to share this with others!

28 ounces white chocolate

1 cup unsalted butter

8 tablespoons corn syrup

3 teaspoons pure peppermint extract

2 cups macadamia nuts

12 candy canes, crushed (plus some more for decorating)

1 cup red M&M's

5 cups mini white marshmallows

1. Place the white chocolate, butter, and corn syrup in a pot over medium-low heat. Stir consistently until completely melted. Then add the peppermint extract. Don't worry if the chocolate and butter have separated.

2. Remove from the heat, and stir the mixture with a spatula or a whisk until the chocolate and butter have fully combined. Add the macadamia nuts, crushed candy canes, red M&M's, and marshmallows and mix until just combined. Pour the mixture into a square 9 × 9–inch aluminum container and sprinkle some extra crushed candy canes on top. Cover with aluminum foil and place this in the freezer until set.

3. Slice the rocky road fudge into bite-sized squares, and you're done!

Red and Green Striped Marshmallows

MAKES ABOUT 25 MARSHMALLOWS

These marshmallows are amazingly soft and infinitely better than store-bought marshmallows! For an extra fancy touch, replace the vanilla extract with seeds from two vanilla beans. It will add an amazing fragrance to the marshmallows that you don't get when just using the extract!

Cooking spray
⅔ cup + ½ cup cold water
5 teaspoons powdered gelatin
2 cups granulated sugar
2 teaspoons vanilla extract
Red and green food coloring

Coating:
¼ cup cornstarch
¼ cup confectioners' sugar

1. Line a 9 × 9–inch square cake pan with parchment paper and grease the paper.

2. Pour ⅔ cup of cold water into the bowl of an electric mixer and sprinkle the powdered gelatin on top. Let sit for 5 minutes.

3. Place the sugar and ½ cup cold water in a small pot and set to medium-high heat. Stir until the sugar has melted.

4. Attach a candy thermometer to the pot and boil the sugar until it reaches 238°F. Brush the sides of the pot with a wet pastry brush if sugar crystals stick to the sides. Add the vanilla extract and mix well.

5. Add the hot sugar to the gelatin and stir the mixture by hand whisking for a few minutes to slightly cool. Then beat with an electric mixer on medium-high speed for about 15 minutes, until soft peaks form.

6. At this point, you need to work quickly because the marshmallow will set quickly. Divide the marshmallow into two bowls. Dye one bowl green and the other red. Place both colors into piping bags and snip off the ends to create large holes. You don't need to be too exact here, which is why piping tips are unnecessary.

7. Pipe the marshmallow into the dish in a diagonal pattern, alternating the colors. One you've piped one layer of stripes, pipe another layer directly on top.

8. Allow the marshmallow to set overnight, until firm.

9. Combine the cornstarch and confectioners' sugar in a bowl. Scoop it into a mesh sieve and dust it over the entire surface of the marshmallow. Gently remove the marshmallow from the pan and place it on a surface that has also been generously dusted in that mixture.

10. Use a sharp knife to cut off the uneven edges of the marshmallow. You may need to dust the knife in the powder if it gets too sticky. Cut the marshmallow into 1-inch cubes and dust all the sticky sides in the powder.

11. Store in an airtight container for 2 to 3 days.

HOMEMADE MINI MARSHMALLOWS

MAKES ABOUT 3 CUPS

If you want to be the most fabulous host, you simply must serve your hot chocolate with homemade mini marshmallows! And the fun part is that you can add any flavoring or coloring that you like!

⅓ cup + ¼ cup cold water
2½ teaspoons powdered gelatin
1 cup granulated sugar
1 teaspoon vanilla extract

Coating:
¼ cup cornstarch
¼ cup confectioners' sugar

1. Line two large baking sheets with parchment paper. Set aside.

2. Pour ⅓ cup of cold water into the bowl of an electric mixer and sprinkle the powdered gelatin on top. Let sit for 5 minutes.

3. Place the sugar and ¼ cup cold water in a small pot and set to medium-high heat. Stir until the sugar has melted.

4. Attach a candy thermometer to the pot and boil the sugar until it reaches 238°F. Brush the sides of the pot with a wet pastry brush if sugar crystals stick to the sides. Add the vanilla extract and mix well.

5. Add the hot sugar to the gelatin and stir the mixture by hand whisking for a few minutes to slightly cool. Then beat with an electric mixer on medium-high speed for about 15 minutes, until soft peaks form.

6. Place the marshmallow into a piping bag fitted with a medium, round piping tip.

7. Pipe long, even stripes of marshmallow onto the baking sheets. Allow the marshmallow to set for 3 to 4 hours, or until firm.

8. Combine the cornstarch and confectioners' sugar in a bowl. Scoop it into a mesh sieve and dust it over the entire surface of the marshmallows.

9. Use a sharp knife to cut the marshmallow into 1-centimeter-long pieces. Dust with more powder.

10. Store the marshmallows in an airtight container and use within 2 to 3 days.

Meringue Christmas Trees

MAKES ABOUT 12 MERINGUES

Light, crispy meringue trees with a chewy middle!

4 large egg whites, room temperature
½ teaspoon cream of tartar
Pinch of salt
1 cup granulated sugar
1 teaspoon vanilla extract or paste
Green food coloring
Sprinkles

1. Preheat the oven to 225°F. Line a large cookie sheet with parchment paper and set aside.

2. Place the egg whites, cream of tartar, and salt into a large mixing bowl. Beat with an electric mixer on low speed until the eggs look foamy. The mixing bowl and the whisks must be completely clean and grease-free, as the egg whites will not whip otherwise.

3. Increase the speed to high and add the granulated sugar 1 tablespoon at a time, until all of the sugar has been added and is dissolved. You'll know that the sugar has dissolved if you rub a small amount of meringue between your fingers and do not feel any graininess. Beat until the meringue is thick, glossy, and holds stiff peaks. Add the vanilla extract and green food coloring and gently stir to combine.

4. Place the meringue into a piping bag fitted with a large, star-shaped piping tip.

5. Pipe swirls of meringue onto the baking sheet, trying to make as tall a swirl as possible. Gently scatter sprinkles on top.

6. Bake them for 1 hour. Once they've finished baking, do not open the oven. Keep them in the oven with the door closed for 2 hours, until they are cooled completely. They will be crisp and will easily peel off from the parchment paper.

7. Store them in an airtight container and enjoy!

CHRISTMAS POPCORN BALLS

MAKES 24 BALLS

A delicious mix between popcorn and crispy rice squares! Because the hot sugar mixture needs to be poured onto the popcorn immediately, I like to make two batches: one red and one green. If you find that this is too many popcorn balls, this recipe can easily be cut in half!

4 quarts (2 bags) popped popcorn
2 cups mini marshmallows
1 cup granulated sugar
1 cup light corn syrup
¼ cup water
¼ teaspoon salt
3 tablespoons unsalted butter
1 teaspoon vanilla extract
Red or green food coloring
Cooking spray (optional, but handy)

1. Place the popcorn and marshmallows on a large baking sheet and mix until the marshmallows are evenly dispersed. Set aside.

2. Pour the sugar, corn syrup, water, and salt into a pot. Set to medium heat and cook until the mixture reaches soft-ball stage, 235°F.

3. Remove the pot from the heat and add the butter, vanilla extract, and food coloring. Stir until everything is incorporated. Immediately pour the sugar mixture onto the popcorn, stirring until evenly combined.

4. Once the mixture is cool enough to handle, shape it into balls. If your hands are sticking to the popcorn, coat them in a thin layer of cooking spray. Enjoy!

Minty Christmas Tree Fudge

MAKES ABOUT 12 (4-INCH) TREES

The softest, creamiest fudge you'll ever make! Not a fan of white chocolate? Replace it with milk chocolate, and it will be just as delicious!

3 cups white chocolate
½ cup unsalted butter
¼ cup light corn syrup
2 teaspoons vanilla extract
3 teaspoons pure peppermint extract
Pinch of salt
Green food coloring
5 cups mini white marshmallows
½ cup macadamia nuts
½ cup gummy candies
¼ cup red melting wafers
12 pieces yellow taffy candy

1. Place the white chocolate, butter, and corn syrup in a pot over medium-low heat. Stir consistently until completely melted. Then add the vanilla and peppermint extract and salt. Don't worry if the chocolate and butter have separated. Add a couple drops of green food coloring. Then add the marshmallows and mix until they are about 50 percent melted.

2. Remove from the heat and stir the mixture with a spatula or a whisk until the chocolate and butter have fully combined. Add the macadamia nuts and gummies and mix until just combined.

3. Pour the mixture into a silicone Christmas tree–shaped mold. Place this in the fridge to set, about 2 hours.

4. Unmold and decorate the trees with dollops of red melting wafers to look like ornaments. Shape stars out of the yellow taffy and place them at the tops of the trees.

5. This fudge will soften quickly, so store it in an airtight container in the fridge.

GINGERBREAD MAN MERINGUE POPS

These cookies taste wonderfully of gingerbread and are a fun twist on the classic gingerbread man!

4 large egg whites, room temperature
½ teaspoon cream of tartar
Pinch of salt
1 cup granulated sugar
1 teaspoon vanilla extract or paste
Brown food coloring
½ teaspoon Gingerbread Spice Mix
   (page 93)
Cookie pop sticks
Mini chocolate chips
Red and green candies

1. Preheat the oven to 225°F. Line a large cookie sheet with parchment paper and set aside.

2. Place the egg whites, cream of tartar, and salt into a large mixing bowl. Beat with an electric mixer on low speed until the eggs look foamy. The mixing bowl and the whisks must be completely clean and grease-free, as the egg whites will not whip otherwise.

3. Increase the speed to high and add the granulated sugar 1 tablespoon at a time, until all of the sugar has been added and is dissolved. You'll know that the sugar has dissolved if you rub a small amount of meringue between your fingers and do not feel any graininess. Beat until the meringue is thick, glossy, and holds stiff peaks. Add the vanilla extract and gently stir to combine.

4. Place ⅓ cup of the meringue into a piping bag fitted with a small, round piping tip. Set aside.

5. Add a couple drops of brown food coloring and the Gingerbread Spice Mix to the remaining meringue and gently stir to combine. If you feel like the meringue has deflated slightly, beat it for a little longer with the electric mixer. Place this meringue into a piping bag fitted with a large, round piping tip.

6. Arrange the cookie pop sticks onto your cookie sheet and pipe gingerbread man shapes onto the sticks. I piped a large dollop for the head, arms, and legs and then joined them together in the middle. Use the white meringue to pipe the icing accents onto the cookies. Use mini chocolate chips as the eyes and red and green candies as the buttons.

7. Bake them for 1 hour. Once they've finished baking, do not open the oven. Keep them in the oven with the door closed for 2 hours, until they are cooled completely. They will be crisp and will easily peel up from the parchment paper.

8. Store them in an airtight container and enjoy!

TURKEY MARSHMALLOWS

If you're looking for a unique holiday treat, this is absolutely it! When serving, "baste" them with some of your hot chocolate to make them glisten and glow. You could also package these in individual cellophane bags and use them as adorable stocking stuffer treats!

Marshmallow Base:
⅓ cup cold water + ¼ cup cold water, divided
2½ teaspoons powdered gelatin
1 cup sugar
1 teaspoon vanilla extract
½ teaspoon ground cinnamon
Brown food coloring
40 mini marshmallows (2 per turkey)
¼ cup cocoa powder

1. Pour ⅓ cup of cold water into the bowl of an electric mixer and sprinkle the powdered gelatin on top. Let sit for 5 minutes.

2. Place the sugar and ¼ cup cold water in a small pot and set to medium-high heat. Stir until the sugar has melted.

3. Attach a candy thermometer to the pot and boil the sugar until it reaches 238°F. Brush the sides of the pot with a wet pastry brush if sugar crystals stick to the sides. Remove the pot from the heat and stir until the sugar stops boiling.

4. Add the hot sugar to the gelatin and stir the mixture by hand whisking for a few minutes to slightly cool. Then beat with an electric mixer on medium-high speed for 8 to 10 minutes, until soft peaks form. Add the vanilla extract, ground cinnamon, and a couple drops of brown food coloring. Beat for another 1 minute, until everything is fully combined

5. Place ¾ of the marshmallow mixture into a piping bag fitted with a large, round piping tip. Place the remaining marshmallow into a piping bag fitted with a small/medium-sized round piping tip.

6. Line a baking sheet with parchment paper. Using the piping bag fitted with the large piping tip, pipe oval mounds that will become the turkey's body. Once you have piped all of the bodies, pipe the legs using

(Continued on page 122)

the piping bag fitted with the small/medium round piping tip. Pipe the thigh first, then pull the piping bag upward to create the base of the leg.

7. Once the turkeys are fully piped, stick a mini marshmallow to the base of each turkey's leg.

8. Leave the marshmallows at room temperature for 6 hours, or up to overnight, until the surface of the marshmallows is only slightly sticky and the marshmallows have firmed up.

9. Take a pastry brush and dust the turkeys with cocoa powder. Dust off any excess cocoa powder, then gently remove the marshmallows from the baking sheet with the help of a butter knife or an offset spatula. Gently dust more cocoa powder onto the sticky base.

10. To serve, place a turkey into your mug of hot chocolate and "baste" them! This will give the turkeys their freshly roasted glow! These turkeys are best consumed immediately or the next day. You can store them in an airtight container at room temperature.

Note: You could also use an egg-shaped silicone mold to shape the bodies of the turkeys! Be sure to spray it with cooking spray and make a second batch of marshmallow for the legs, which will be piped after the marshmallow has set for 6 hours and unmolded onto a sheet of parchment paper.

Hot Chocolate Gummy Bears

MAKES 3 DOZEN

Sweet, creamy, and very portable! Enjoy your favorite holiday drink in gummy bear form!

1 cup cold water
½ cup powdered gelatin
1 cup sweetened condensed milk
¼ cup sugar
1 teaspoon vanilla extract
¼ cup cocoa powder

1. Pour the water and gelatin into a pot and let sit for 10 minutes, until the gelatin has developed.

2. Set the pot to medium high heat and whisk until the gelatin has dissolved. Add the condensed milk, sugar, and vanilla extract and whisk until fully combined. Sift the cocoa powder into the mixture and whisk until fully combined. If you find that there are still pieces of undissolved cocoa powder, you can pour the liquid through a mesh sieve.

3. Pour the mixture into a gummy bear mold then transfer to the fridge and allow the gummy bears to set, about 1 hour.

4. Unmold the gummy bears and enjoy! To store, place the gummy bears in an airtight container and store in the fridge.

Snowglobe Lollipops

MAKES ABOUT 48 (1.5-INCH) LOLLIPOPS

The most giftable holiday treat in this book! Perfect for classmates, coworkers, stocking stuffers, or even handing out to neighbors! I used peppermint extract, but you can use whatever flavoring you like. Be sure to do so sparingly, as other flavorings are usually far more potent than vanilla and peppermint extract, so start with just a couple drops. This recipe can easily be divided in half!

Lollipops:
2½ cups granulated sugar
1 cup water
1½ cups light corn syrup
1 teaspoon vanilla extract
½ teaspoon peppermint extract
Cooking spray
48 lollipop sticks

Decorations:
1 cup white chocolate, melted
½ cup red sanding sugar
½ cup dark chocolate, melted
¼ cup orange melting wafers, melted

Make the Lollipops:

1. Set a pot over medium heat and add the granulated sugar, water, and light corn syrup. Stir with a rubber spatula until everything is melted and combined. Then increase the heat to medium-high and attach a candy thermometer to the pot. Heat the sugar until it reaches 310°F.

2. Remove the pot from the heat and stir until it stops bubbling. Add the vanilla and peppermint extract and mix until fully combined.

3. Use a ladle to pour the candy into a lollipop mold. If using a silicone mold, you can pour the candy right in. If using a hard plastic mold, be sure to spray the mold with cooking spray first. This will prevent the candy from sticking.

4. Stick lollipop sticks into the candy and rotate them several times to ensure that they are covered in the candy. This will secure them to the candy.

5. Leave the lollipops at room temperature for 2 to 3 hours, until fully cooled and hardened. Then unmold and set aside.

Decorate:

1. Spread some white chocolate onto the base of each lollipop, then dip it into the red sanding sugar. This will create the "base" of the snowglobes. Let harden at room temperature, about 30 minutes.

2. Place the white chocolate into a piping bag and snip a small hole at the tip. Pipe the body of the snowman onto the middle of the lollipops.

3. Using a toothpick and the remaining white chocolate, make little dots all around the sides of the snowman to look like snow.

4. Use another toothpick and the dark chocolate to draw the snowman's eyes, buttons, and arms. Then draw the snowman's nose with the orange melting wafers and a third toothpick.

5. These lollipops should be stored at room temperature and consumed within 2 weeks.

"Crispy" Turkey

I'm certain that this is the sort of turkey served for Christmas dinner at Santa's workshop!

6 tablespoons unsalted butter
2¼ cups chocolate chips
8 cups mini marshmallows
11 cups crispy rice cereal
2 small sheets of white paper
¼ cup gummies

1. Melt the butter in a large pan set to low heat. Add the chocolate chips and melt. Add the mini marshmallows and mix until fully melted and combined.

2. Remove from the heat and add the cereal. Gently fold together until they are fully coated in the chocolate.

3. Transfer the crispy rice treats to a large, buttered baking sheet. Using clean hands, shape two thirds of the treats into the turkey's body. Make the drumsticks and wings out of the remaining treats and stick these onto the body. Place the baking sheet in the fridge for 30 minutes for the turkey to set.

4. Make little white toppers for the drumsticks by folding a small sheet of paper in half and cutting slits through the folded side with scissors. Wrap the paper around the end of a drumstick and trim off any excess paper. Tape the ends together to form a ring, and slide onto the end of the drumstick. Repeat with the other sheet of paper.

5. Place the turkey on a serving platter and fill the turkey's cavity with fruit gummies and enjoy!

DRINKS

Snickerdoodle Hot Chocolate

SERVES 2

There's not much better than cookie-infused hot chocolate! I absolutely encourage you to try this out with other cookies. Chocolate chip cookies or sugar cookies would be absolutely delicious.

Snickerdoodle Base:
6 Snickerdoodles (page 60)
2 cups milk

Hot Chocolate:
2 cups milk
¾ cup milk chocolate
½ teaspoon vanilla extract

Topping:
¾ cup whipping cream
1 teaspoon ground cinnamon
2 tablespoons confectioners' sugar
Crushed snickerdoodle pieces

Make the Snickerdoodle Base:

1. Combine the Snickerdoodles and 2 cups milk in a pot and set to medium heat.

2. Bring to a boil, then remove the pan from the heat and allow the milk to cool to room temperature. The milk will thicken, but don't worry!

3. Pour the mixture through a cheesecloth into a dish. Set aside.

Make the Hot Chocolate:

1. Pour 2 cups milk, the milk chocolate pieces, vanilla extract, and the snickerdoodle base into a pot. Set to medium heat and whisk until everything is melted and well combined. Remove from the heat and set aside.

Make the Topping:

1. Place the whipping cream, cinnamon, and confectioners' sugar in a bowl and beat with an electric mixer until stiff peaks form.

2. Place in a piping bag fitted with a large, star-shaped piping tip.

Assembly:

1. Pour the hot chocolate into mugs and top with a swirl of whipped cream. Sprinkle some snickerdoodle crumbs on top and enjoy!

Eggnog Hot Chocolate

SERVES 2-4

Simple, but creamy and delicious! I used white chocolate in keeping with the creamy theme of this hot chocolate, but you can definitely use milk or dark chocolate instead.

4 cups eggnog
1 cup white chocolate
1 teaspoon vanilla extract
Whipped cream
Ground nutmeg
Cinnamon stick

1. Pour the eggnog, white chocolate, and vanilla extract into a pot over medium heat. Stir constantly until the white chocolate has fully melted.

2. Pour the hot chocolate into your desired mugs and top with whipped cream. Sprinkle some nutmeg on top and decorate with a cinnamon stick!

Hot Chocolate Bombs

MAKES 1 BOMB

A holiday classic! Pop one into your favorite mug, pour in some hot milk, and watch it melt into hot chocolaty goodness!

1 (3.5-ounce) dark, milk, or white chocolate bar
1 tablespoon mini marshmallows
1 tablespoon cocoa powder
2 tablespoons sugar
1 teaspoon festive sprinkles
1–2 cups hot milk

1. Break the chocolate into small pieces and place it in a microwave-safe bowl. Microwave it for 20- to 30-second intervals, mixing at each interval. The chocolate can also be melted using a double boiler.

2. Fill your mold ¾ of the way full with the chocolate and gently rotate it so that the chocolate coats all sides. Place a sheet of parchment paper onto your work surface. Turn the mold upside down and allow the excess chocolate to drip onto the parchment paper. Scrape the chocolate off the parchment paper and return it to your bowl.

3. Use the flat back of a butter knife to smooth the edges of the chocolate mold. Place the mold in the fridge for 20 to 30 minutes, until the chocolate has fully set.

4. Repeat steps 2 and 3 to create a second layer of chocolate. This will prevent the chocolate shell from breaking during unmolding and assembly. When smoothing the edges of the chocolate mold with the butter knife, ensure that the edges of the shell are 1 to 3 millimeters thick. This will allow both halves to securely stick together in the following steps.

5. Gently unmold the chocolate shells and rest them on a plate or on top of small glasses, which will support the spherical shape very well and keep it from wobbling away.

6. Make the hot chocolate mix by combining the cocoa powder and sugar in a small bowl. Spoon some of the mix into one chocolate shell. You don't have to use all of the mixture. Add some marshmallows and sprinkles, if desired.

7. Remelt some of the remaining melted chocolate and spread it onto the ridges of the filled shell. Place the other shell on top, press gently to seal, and place the hot chocolate bomb into the fridge for 10 minutes, or until the chocolate seal has set.

8. To decorate, drizzle or spread some more chocolate on top. The chocolate should be melted but cooled to room temperature so that it doesn't melt the chocolate shell. Sprinkle some sprinkles on top, if desired. Then chill the hot chocolate bomb in the fridge for another 10 minutes.

9. To serve, drop the hot chocolate bomb into a mug of hot milk. Stir and watch the marshmallow appear!

Strawberry Hot Chocolate

Everything is better when it's pink, and this hot chocolate is no exception! If you can't get your hands on a drink mix like Nesquik, you can use ¼ cup of dehydrated strawberry powder or replace the milk with strawberry milk!

Hot Chocolate:
1½ cups white chocolate
½ cup strawberry drink mix (e.g., Nesquik)
2 cups milk
1 cup whipping cream

Topping:
½ cup whipping cream, cold
1 teaspoon vanilla extract
2 tablespoons confectioners' sugar
¼ cup pink mini marshmallows
¼ cup dehydrated strawberries

1. Place the white chocolate, strawberry drink mix, milk, and 1 cup whipping cream into a pot and set to medium heat.

2. Stir until the chocolate has melted and everything is mixed together.

3. To decorate, place ½ cup whipping cream in a bowl and add the vanilla extract and confectioners' sugar. Beat with an electric mixer until stiff peaks form. Place the cream in a piping bag fitted with a large, star-shaped piping tip.

4. Pour the hot chocolate into mugs and pipe a swirl of whipped cream on top. Top with pink marshmallows and a dehydrated strawberry slice. You can also crumble the dehydrated strawberries in your hands to create a beautiful pink "dust"!

Snowflake Hot Chocolate Melts

You will need a snowflake-shaped silicone mold (or ice cube tray) for this recipe. Each cavity should have a rough capacity of 3 tablespoons.

1½ cups good-quality white chocolate, melted

¾ cup dark chocolate, melted

2 teaspoons butterfly pea powder

⅓ cup ruby chocolate, melted

¼ cup marshmallow bits

1. Place your snowflake mold on a tray that will fit into your fridge. Fill the cavities one third of the way with white chocolate and tap the tray on the counter a couple times to flatten the surface. Place the tray in the fridge for 15 minutes.

2. Pour the dark chocolate on top, filling the cavities another one third of the way full. Smooth the surface and return to the fridge for 15 minutes, until the dark chocolate has set.

3. Add the butterfly pea powder to the remaining white chocolate and pour this into half of the cavities. Pour the ruby chocolate into the remaining cavities. Sprinkle the marshmallow bits on top and gently press them into the chocolate to ensure they stick.

4. Return the mold to the fridge for about 30 minutes, for the chocolate to fully set.

5. Unmold and admire your beautiful snowflakes! To serve, place one snowflake in your mug and top with 1 cup of hot milk. Stir to melt the snowflake and enjoy.

NOTE: Because we did not temper the chocolate in this recipe, these snowflakes will need to be stored in an airtight container in the fridge or freezer.

Peppermint Frozen Hot Chocolate

If you're a fan of cold drinks in cold weather, this is for you! The addition of melted chocolate brings this milkshake to the next level and makes it even more indulgent.

¼ **cup melted white chocolate (+ extra for decorating the glass)**
¼ **cup crushed candy canes**
3 **tablespoons warm milk**
2 **cups candy cane or mint chocolate chip ice cream**
½ **cup cold milk**
Whipped cream
Whole candy canes
Festive straws

1. First, decorate the glasses. Drizzle some white chocolate onto the inside of two chilled glasses. Spread some melted white chocolate along the rims. Immediately sprinkle some crushed candy canes onto the chocolate and place them in the freezer for the chocolate to set while you make the milkshake.

2. In a small bowl, combine the melted ¼ cup of white chocolate and warm milk. Add this to a blender along with some candy cane ice cream and cold milk. Blend until smooth.

3. Pour into the glasses and top with some whipped cream and extra crushed candy canes. Garnish with a full candy cane and festive straw. Enjoy!

Hot Chocolate Pigs

MAKES 10 (1-INCH) PIGS (ENOUGH FOR ABOUT 3 CUPS OF HOT CHOCOLATE)

The most adorable stocking stuffer or gift for classmates, these sweet little bags contain enough ingredients to make 3 cups of hot chocolate. When gifting, add directions to the tag to melt the pigs in 3 cups of hot milk.

1 (3.5-ounce) chocolate bar (any flavor)
2 tablespoons marshmallow bits
Festive sprinkles
Marshmallow bits

1. Place the chocolate in a microwave-safe bowl and microwave for 20- to 30-second intervals until melted, stirring at each interval.

2. Pour the chocolate into a pig-shaped silicone mold. Top the chocolates with 2 tablespoons of marshmallow bits. Gently press the marshmallow bits into the chocolate so that they stick.

3. Place the mold in the fridge for 30 minutes, until the chocolate has set.

4. Fill cellophane bags with a scoop of sprinkles and a scoop of marshmallow bits, then top with some chocolate pigs. Tie the bags closed and enjoy!

ORNAMENT PUNCH

MAKES 4 CUPS

This punch is instantly turned festive with these adorable glass ornaments used as glasses! Arrange them on your dining room table or hand them out for after school snacks! As tempting as it would be to hang these on your Christmas tree, they get a little heavy and I'm not confident that the hooks will still stay attached. And you deserve to have a Christmas tree skirt that ISN'T covered in punch!

1 cup grapefruit juice
1½ cup orange juice
1½ cup ginger ale
⅓ cup Simple Syrup (page 95)
Red or green food coloring
Red, green, or gold edible glitter

1. Combine the grapefruit juice, orange juice, ginger ale, and Simple Syrup in a bowl.

2. If making all three colors, divide the punch between three bowls. To one bowl, add a couple drops of red food coloring and ½ teaspoon of red edible glitter. For the green punch, add green food coloring and ½ teaspoon of green edible glitter. For the gold, simply add ½ teaspoon of gold edible glitter. Mix very well.

3. Use a small funnel to fill the ornaments and place the hooks back on. The punch will need to be gently swirled or agitated to see the ripples of glitter, so make sure to tell your guests to swirl their ornaments occasionally!

FROZEN POND SODA

This soda may look cold and wintery, but close your eyes and you'll be transported to the tropics!

¼ **batch Classic Royal Icing (page 93), for the rim of the glasses**
1 **cup pineapple juice**
1 **cup lychee juice**
½ **cup coconut cream**
½ **teaspoon vanilla extract**
Blue food coloring
2 **scoops of vanilla ice cream**

1. Dip the rims of two glasses into the Classic Royal Icing. Set aside.

2. Combine the pineapple juice, lychee juice, coconut cream, vanilla extract, and blue food coloring in a pitcher. Mix well.

3. Pour the soda between the glasses. Add a scoop of vanilla ice cream to each glass and serve!

Hot Chocolate Bunny Bombs

If classic hot chocolate bombs aren't rich enough to your taste, try these! These bunnies are filled with homemade chocolate ganache, which will give your hot chocolate a significantly creamier, more luxurious taste. These are also insanely giftable and can be wrapped in cellophane bags for cute, fun Christmas gifts!

2½ cups melted chocolate chips

Filling:
3 cups good-quality dark or milk
    chocolate, finely chopped
½ cup whipping cream, hot
Pinch of salt
¼ cup white chocolate chips, melted
Holly sprinkles

1. Spread the melted chocolate chips onto the inside of an 8-cavity rabbit-shaped silicone mold, creating a chocolate shell. Place the mold in the fridge to set while you make the filling.

2. To make the filling, place the finely chopped chocolate in a bowl and pour the hot whipping cream on top. Allow to sit for 5 minutes, then add the salt and stir until fully combined.

3. Spoon the filling into the bunnies, leaving about ⅛ inch of space. This is important! Return the mold to the fridge for the filling to semi-set, about 20 minutes.

4. Fill the molds the remainder of the way with more melted chocolate chips. This will seal the filling into the bunnies and prevent it from leaking out. This will also create a solid chocolate base so that the bunnies can sit upright! Return the mold to the fridge to finish setting, about 1 hour.

5. Unmold the bunnies. Place a dollop of melted chocolate chips next to the bunny's ear and attach the holly sprinkles.

6. Add a teaspoon of remaining chocolate chips to the ¼ cup white chocolate chips to create a light brown chocolate. Use a skewer or a toothpick to paint on the bunny's eyes and ears with this light brown chocolate.

7. To serve, place a bunny in a pot and add 2 cups of milk. Bring the heat to medium and melt the bunny! You can also do this in a mug in a classic hot chocolate bomb-style with hot milk; however, these bunnies are quite large, so I recommend using one of those mega coffee mugs. But hey, it's the holidays—no one is going to question your bowl of hot chocolate!

SAVORY/BREAKFAST

JUMBO GINGERBREAD MUFFINS

MAKES 8 JUMBO MUFFINS

This muffin recipe is so delicious that my dog, Treacle, tried to sneak a taste while I was photographing them! These muffins aren't dog friendly, but she sure didn't think so!

Muffin Batter:
Cooking spray
½ cup light brown sugar
1 cup molasses
½ cup milk
½ cup liquid coconut oil
2 large eggs, room temperature
4 cups all-purpose flour
4 teaspoons Gingerbread Spice Mix
  (page 93)
2 teaspoons baking soda
½ teaspoon salt
1 apple (I used Honeycrisp), peeled and
  finely chopped
⅓ cup pecans, finely chopped
⅓ cup walnuts, finely chopped

Streusel Topping:
½ cup all-purpose flour
¼ cup light brown sugar, packed
¾ teaspoon Gingerbread Spice Mix
  (page 93)
Pinch of salt
3 tablespoons cold butter, cut into small
  cubes
¼ cup snowflake sprinkles
Gingerbread man icing decorations

1. Preheat the oven to 400°F. Grease a jumbo muffin pan with cooking spray.

2. In a large bowl, use an electric mixer to combine the brown sugar, molasses, milk, oil, and eggs. In a separate bowl, combine the flour, Gingerbread Spice Mix, baking soda, and salt. Add this to the wet mixture and mix until just combined.

3. Fold the apple, pecans, and walnuts into the batter, then divide it into the muffin pan. Set aside while you make the streusel.

4. Whisk together the flour, brown sugar, Gingerbread Spice Mix, and salt in a bowl. Add the butter and incorporate it using two butter knives, "cutting" it into the flour mixture until crumbly but sticks together when pinched.

5. Evenly sprinkle the streusel on top of the muffins. Decorate with the snowflake sprinkles and gingerbread men, then bake for 35 minutes, or until a skewer inserted into the muffins comes out clean. Enjoy your delicious muffins!

Hedgehog Cheese Ball

Cheese boards are all the rage during the holidays, and yours deserves to be the cutest! Surround this little hedgehog with crackers, fresh figs, and grapes for the cutest evening snack you could ask for.

Body:
½ pound (1 cup) cream cheese, room temperature
1 cup cheddar cheese, grated
½ tablespoon Dijon mustard
½ teaspoon Worcestershire sauce
Pinch of pepper
1 cup pecans, finely chopped

Face, Arms, and Feet:
⅓ cup white cheddar, grated
⅓ cup cream cheese, room temperature
⅓ cup goat cheese, room temperature
Pinch of pepper
5 dried cranberries

Make the Body:

1. Mix together both cheeses with a spoon or electric mixer. Then add the Dijon mustard, Worcestershire sauce, pepper, and 2 tablespoons of the pecans and mix well.

2. Lay out a sheet of plastic wrap, and sprinkle on the remaining chopped pecans. Place the cheese mixture on top, and shape it into a large oval. Wrap the cheese in the plastic wrap, and set in the fridge for 30 minutes.

Make the Face, Arms, and Feet:

1. Mix together all of the cheeses, and add the pepper. Place about three quarters of the mixture onto a sheet of plastic wrap, and shape it into the face and snout.

2. Unwrap the body and place it on a serving platter. Unwrap the snout and attach it to the body. Use the remaining goat cheese mixture to create the arms and legs and attach them to the body.

3. Stick some dried cranberries onto the face to create the ears, eyes, and nose.

CHRISTMAS MORNING BANANA BREAD

MAKES 1 (9-INCH) LOAF

This banana bread recipe has been in my family for years and is so moist and not too sweet, making it perfect for breakfast! I love adding extra touches, such as the sprinkles and butterscotch chips in this recipe. If you'd like to make muffins instead, pour the batter into a muffin pan and bake for 15-20 minutes.

Banana Bread:
3 ripe bananas
6 tablespoon vegetable oil
½ cup sugar
1 egg
1 teaspoon vanilla extract
¼ teaspoon salt
1½ cups all-purpose flour
1 teaspoon baking soda
1 teaspoon baking powder
½ cup Homemade Holiday Sprinkles
    (page 103), plus extra for decorating
½ cup butterscotch chips

Glaze:
4 ounces cream cheese, room temperature
¾ cup confectioners' sugar
2 tablespoon milk

1. Preheat the oven to 350°F and grease a 9-inch loaf pan.

2. Combine the bananas, oil and sugar in a large bowl. Then add the egg, vanilla and salt.

3. Mix flour, soda and baking powder together in a separate bowl and add to banana mixture. Add the Homemade Holiday Sprinkles and butterscotch chips and fold to combine.

4. Spoon the batter into the loaf pan and bake for 45 minutes, or until a skewer inserted into the loaf comes out clean. Cool completely.

5. To make the glaze, place the cream cheese and confectioners' sugar in a bowl and mix together. Add the milk and whisk until smooth. Drizzle on top of the banana bread and decorate with additional sprinkles. Then slice and enjoy!

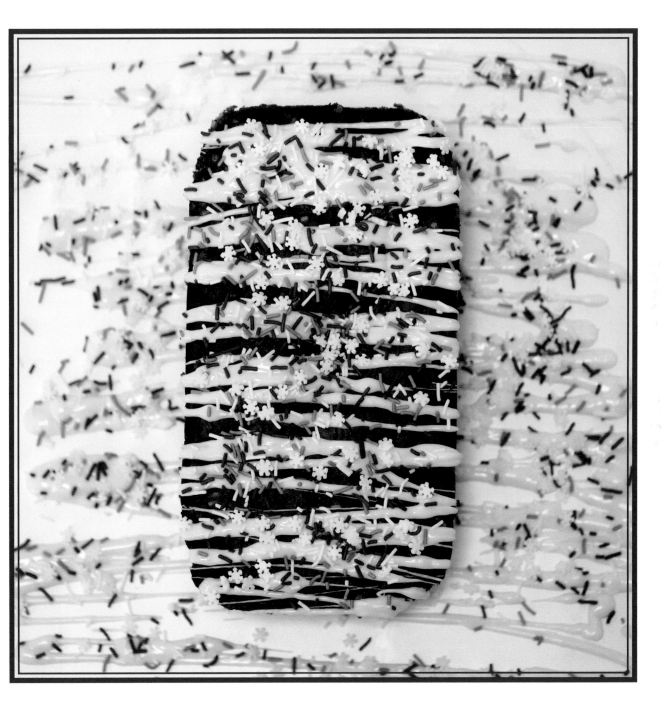

Red and Green Cinnamon Buns

MAKES 14 BUNS

The perfect treat for Christmas morning! These can be started ahead of time and the process resumed at step 10 on the day you wish to serve them!

Brioche:
⅓ cup whole milk, warm
2¼ teaspoon active dry yeast
5 large eggs, room temperature
3½ cups all-purpose flour, divided
⅓ cup granulated sugar
1 teaspoon salt
1½ cups unsalted butter, room temperature, divided in half
Red and green food coloring

Filling:
6 tablespoons granulated sugar
3½ teaspoons ground cinnamon
1 large egg, beaten
¾ cup butter, room temperature

Frosting:
8 ounces cream cheese, room temperature
1½ cups confectioners' sugar
2 tablespoons milk
1 teaspoon vanilla extract
Red and green sprinkles

1. Pour the milk, yeast, 1 egg, and 1 cup flour into the bowl of an electric mixer. Mix to combine, then sprinkle over another 1 cup flour. Let rise for 40 minutes.

2. Add the remaining 4 eggs to the dough, along with the sugar, salt, and 1 more cup of flour. Place these into a mixer fitted with a dough hook and mix on low speed for 2 minutes. Add the remaining ½ cup flour and mix on medium speed for 15 minutes.

3. Reduce the speed to medium-low and gradually add ¾ cup butter. Increase the speed to medium-high and beat for 1 minute, then reduce the speed to medium and beat for 5 minutes.

4. Place the dough in a large, buttered bowl and cover with plastic wrap. Let rise for 2½ hours.

5. Deflate the dough and divide it into two pieces. Dye one ball red and the other green with several drops of food coloring. It may take some time for the food coloring to evenly disperse through the dough, but don't give up! It will happen! Place the balls on a buttered baking sheet and cover with plastic wrap. Let sit at room temperature for 4 to 6 hours, or up to overnight.

6. Divide each ball of dough into 6 pieces and roll them into 10-inch-long sausage shapes. On a floured work surface, arrange 3 red and 3 green sausages side by side, pinching the edges together to create a striped dough. Roll the dough into an 11 × 13–inch

(Continued on page 160)

rectangle. Evenly disperse half of the remaining butter onto the surface of the dough, then fold the dough into thirds, like a letter.

7. Roll the dough out into an 11 × 13–inch rectangle, then fold into thirds again. Wrap it tightly in plastic wrap and place it in the fridge for 30 minutes. Repeat with the remaining dough.

8. Combine the sugar and cinnamon in a bowl and set aside.

9. Place one piece of dough on a floured surface and roll into an 11 × 13–inch rectangle. Brush the surface with the beaten egg. Sprinkle half of the cinnamon sugar onto the dough, leaving the top quarter of the dough bare. Roll the dough into a log, starting with the cinnamon sugar end and ending with the bare end. Wrap in plastic wrap and place in the freezer for 45 minutes. Repeat with the remaining dough. (**Note:** If making these for a particular event, you can complete the previous steps a day in advance and start from step 10 on the day you are serving them.)

10. Divide ¾ cup butter between two 9-inch round baking tins or one 13 × 9–inch rectangular baking dish.

11. Unwrap the logs and slice them into 1½-inch-thick buns, making 14 buns. If using two baking tins, divide the buns between the tins or space them evenly apart in the one tin. Let the buns rise at room temperature for 1½ hours.

12. Preheat the oven to 350°F. Bake the buns for 35 to 40 minutes, until golden brown. Place a baking sheet lined with parchment paper on the rack under the cinnamon buns to catch any drips.

13. As soon as the cinnamon buns are finished baking, flip them out onto a wire rack. Excess butter may drip out, so make sure to place some paper towel under the rack. Turn the buns right side up and let them cool slightly.

14. To make the icing, place the cream cheese in a bowl and beat with an electric mixer for 2 minutes, until the cream cheese is fluffy. Add the confectioners' sugar, milk, and vanilla extract and mix until combined.

15. Spread the frosting onto the cinnamon buns and decorate with sprinkles.

WREATH BAGELS

MAKES 10 BAGELS

Homemade bread always feels like such a treat and these bagels are feeling extra festive! If you're not up to braiding them, you can simply make a ring of dough and they'll be just as delicious!

2¼ cups warm water, divided
2¼ teaspoon active dry yeast
2 tablespoons sugar
3 tablespoons vegetable shortening
1 tablespoon salt
Green food coloring
6 cups bread flour
2 tablespoons melted butter
¼ cup sugar
1 teaspoon baking soda
Cooking spray
Sesame seeds, divided
2 large egg whites
1 teaspoon cold water

1. Pour ¼ cup of warm water into the bowl of an electric mixer and sprinkle the yeast on top. Let sit for 5 minutes for the yeast to develop. Add the remaining 2 cups warm water, sugar, vegetable shortening, a couple drops of green food coloring, and salt and mix on low speed with a dough hook attachment.

2. Gradually add 5½ cups of bread flour, mixing for 2 to 3 minutes until all ingredients are combined. Increase to medium speed and mix for 6 minutes, adding the remaining flour 1 tablespoon at a time.

3. Brush the inside of a large bowl with some of the melted butter. Shape the dough into a ball and place inside the bowl. Brush the top of the bread with some more butter and cover with a sheet of buttered plastic wrap. Place a towel on top and let the dough rise at room temperature for 1 hour.

4. Deflate the dough, return to the bowl, cover, and chill in the fridge for 4 hours, or overnight.

5. In the meantime, do some prep. Spray two baking sheets with cooking spray and sprinkle sesame seeds on top. Cover two additional baking sheets with dish towels and sprinkle flour onto one of the dish towels. Set aside.

6. Transfer the dough to a floured surface. Deflate the dough and divide into 10 pieces. Working with one piece at a time, divide the ball of dough into 3 pieces. Roll all 3 pieces into 9-inch-long sausages, then braid

(Continued on page 162)

them together. You can press the ends of the sausages onto your work surface to stick, which will make braiding them much easier! Once you have a braid of dough, join the ends together to create a braided ring. Transfer the bagel to the baking sheet with the floured dish towel and cover with an additional dish towel. Repeat with the remaining 9 balls of dough.

7. Bring a large pot of water to boil and add the sugar and baking soda. Place the bagels into the boiling water and boil for 1½ to 2 minutes, then flip over and boil for an additional 1½ to 2 minutes on the other side. Transfer the boiled bagels to the baking sheet lined with the un-floured dish towel. Then transfer the bagels to one of the baking sheets sprinkled with sesame seeds. Cover the bagels with a sheet of aluminum foil. This is important, because otherwise the bagels with brown and they won't look green after baking!

8. Preheat the oven to 500°F. If using a gas oven, insert an empty cast-iron pan on the bottom. While the oven is preheating, beat the egg whites and water in a small bowl. Brush the bagels with this glaze, and if desired, sprinkle with additional sesame seeds.

9. In a small glass, place 4 ice cubes and ¼ cup water.

10. Place the bagels in the oven and immediately toss the ice cubes and water onto the oven floor if it's electric. If using a gas oven, toss cubes and water into the hot cast-iron pan placed earlier. Quickly close the oven door and reduce the oven temperature to 450°F. Bake for 25 minutes. Turn off the oven and keep the bagels in the oven for an additional 5 minutes. Then open the oven door and leave the bagels in the oven for another 5 minutes.

11. After cooking, transfer the bagels to a cooling rack and cool completely. Tie a festive ribbon around each bagel and enjoy!

CRANBERRY CHOCOLATE CHIP MUFFINS

The tartness of the cranberries is complemented beautifully by the white and dark chocolate chips!

1¾ cups all-purpose flour
2 teaspoons baking powder
2 teaspoons cornstarch
½ teaspoon salt
¼ cup unsalted butter, melted
¼ cup liquid coconut oil
1 cup granulated sugar
1 large egg
1 large egg white
1½ teaspoons vanilla bean paste
⅓ cup buttermilk
1½ cups frozen cranberries
⅓ cup chopped white chocolate
¼ cup mini semisweet chocolate chips

1. Preheat the oven to 350°F. Line a muffin pan with muffin liners.

2. In a medium-sized bowl, combine the flour, baking powder, cornstarch, and salt.

3. In a large bowl, combine the butter, coconut oil, and granulated sugar with an electric mixer until well combined. Add the egg, egg white, vanilla bean paste, and buttermilk and mix until combined. Add the dry ingredients and whisk until just combined.

4. Add the cranberries, white chocolate, and chocolate chips and fold into the batter until evenly combined.

5. Spoon the batter into the muffin pan and bake for 15 to 20 minutes, or until a skewer inserted into the center comes out clean. Cool completely and enjoy!

CHRISTMAS MORNING OATMEAL

SERVES 2

The most adorable and festive way to enjoy Christmas morning! These don't take too long to whip up, which makes them perfect for a family breakfast if you double the recipe. The brown sugar and coconut cream taste fantastic together and slightly offset the tang of the cranberries, making a unique but still festive breakfast!

1 cup old-fashioned rolled oats

2 cups water

Pinch of salt

½ cup frozen cranberries

¼ cup coconut cream, plus extra for serving

½ kiwi, peeled and sliced into semicircles

2 (½-inch) squares of mango, cut into star shapes

2 squares hazelnut chocolate bar

White sprinkles

Brown sugar for sweetening, if desired

1. Place the oats, water, salt, and cranberries in a pot and set to medium heat.

2. Stir constantly for 10 minutes, until the oatmeal has absorbed the water and softened. Add the coconut cream and mix well.

3. Pour the oatmeal into two bowls.

4. Place the kiwi slices onto the oatmeal in an overlapping pattern to create a Christmas tree shape. Stick the mango star on top and the hazelnut chocolate at the base as the trunk.

5. Scatter some white sprinkles around the tree as snow!

6. Serve the oatmeal alongside brown sugar and coconut cream.

Pine Tree Scones

Serve these scones alongside some tea or hot chocolate after a day of playing in the snow!

¾ cup cake flour
1¼ cups bread flour
1 teaspoon matcha green tea powder
2 teaspoons baking powder
¼ cup unsalted butter, cold and diced
2 tablespoons sugar
1 cup white chocolate chips
½ cup milk (add more if necessary)
Green food coloring
Dark chocolate squares
3 tablespoons confectioners' sugar
¼ cup cream cheese, room temperature
½ tablespoon milk

1. Preheat the oven to 425°F.

2. Sift the cake flour, bread flour, matcha green tea powder, and baking powder.

3. Add the butter and mix with your fingers until it is crumbly in texture. Add the sugar and white chocolate and combine.

4. Dye the milk green with the green food coloring. Add enough milk to the dough for it to come together into a ball.

5. Turn the dough out onto a floured surface and shape into a disk. Cut it into 6 wedges and arrange them on a baking sheet lined with parchment paper.

6. Bake for 15 to 20 minutes. Transfer to a cooling rack and cool completely.

7. Slice a small opening into the base of each triangle and insert a dark chocolate square to create the trunk.

8. Combine the confectioners' sugar, cream cheese, and milk in a bowl, then drizzle on top of the trees to look like snow.

Reindeer Toast

The combination of peanut butter and honey creates a very smooth, sweet spread that is a touch unique compared to the usual peanut butter toast. If you have a busy morning ahead of you, the antlers can be prepped the night before (make sure to not forget the lemon juice!) and stored in an airtight container in the fridge.

3 apple slices
Juice from ½ lemon
3 bread slices or English muffins
⅓ cup peanut butter
2 tablespoons honey
6 blueberries
3 raspberries

1. Use a sharp knife to cut antler shapes out of the slices of apple. If you have a reindeer cookie cutter, you could also just use the antler portion of the cutter to make these antlers! Squeeze lemon juice onto the apple to prevent it from browning.

2. Place the bread in the toaster. While the bread is toasting, mix together the peanut butter and honey.

3. Spread the peanut butter spread onto the toast. Stick 2 antlers onto each piece of toast, along with 2 blueberries for the eyes and one raspberry for the nose.

Note: If you have dogs, beware, because I was wildly harassed as I tried to eat this while sitting on the couch. The honey, peanut butter, and apple combination is apparently very tempting to pups!

The Perfect Gingerbread House, page 175

GINGERBREAD

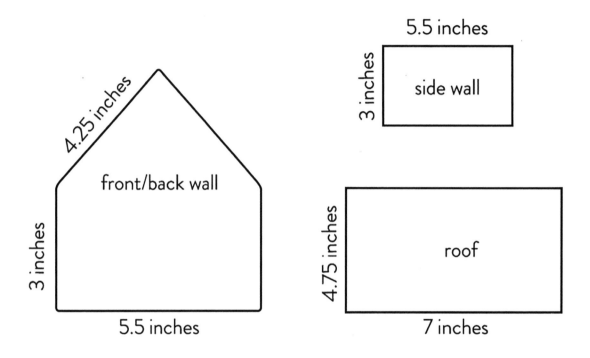

5.5 inches

3 inches

side wall

4.25 inches

front/back wall

3 inches

5.5 inches

4.75 inches

roof

7 inches

make 2 of each shape

THE PERFECT GINGERBREAD HOUSE

Classic, adorable, and featuring the cutest hatched roof! I'm obsessed! This gingerbread is also so fragrant, you'll get a delicious whiff of gingerbread whenever you walk past it.

1 batch Classic Gingerbread Cookies dough (page 71)
1 batch Classic Royal Icing (page 93)
Red and green food coloring
¼ cup holly sprinkles
2½ cups wheat squares cereal (e.g., Chex or Shreddies)

Bake the walls:

1. Preheat the oven to 350°F.

2. Roll the dough out on a floured surface to ¼-inch thick. Follow the guide provided on the opposite page to measure out the front, back, 2 sides, and 2 roof panels of the house.

3. Place the cookies on 2 baking sheets lined with parchment paper. Place the baking sheets in the fridge for about 15 minutes, for the cookies to stiffen. This will prevent the cookies from spreading and becoming misshapen while baking.

4. Bake the cookies for 12 to 15 minutes, until the edges begin to darken. Allow the cookies to cool completely on the baking sheets so that they stay flat.

(Continued on page 176)

Decorate:

1. Place the Classic Royal Icing into a piping bag fitted with a small, round piping tip.

2. Pipe the foundational parts of the decorating first—the stripes, the windows, etc. Then get creative with what you'd like to decorate! I used some extra icing to glue some holly under each window. I then dyed some of the icing a matching green to the sprinkles, placed it in a piping bag fitted with a small, round piping tip, and piped a wreath on the front of the house and a garland on the back of the house, then added little red sprinkles as berries.

3. To make the door, I used a knife to spread a thin layer of red icing into a rectangular shape, then allowed it to dry. I used the same red icing and a piping bag fitted with a small, round piping tip to pipe the border of the door and the 4 rectangular panels. I used some extra white icing for the door handle.

4. For the bushes, I simply used a piping bag fitted with a medium-sized star-shaped piping tip and piped little dollops!

5. Do not decorate the roof panels at this stage!

Assembly:

1. Use the Classic Royal Icing to glue one wall panel to the front house panel. Hold it in place for a couple seconds, then gently release and wait 10 minutes. Add the other wall panel and glue it to the front house panel. Wait 30 minutes for the icing to harden.

2. Pipe some more icing onto the open ends of the wall panels and attach the back house panel. Hold in place for a couple minutes, then allow the icing to harden for about 1 hour.

3. You can also pipe additional icing along the seams of the house for extra support once they begin to stick together.

4. Once the bottom walls feel secure, pipe more icing onto the diagonal sides of the front and back panels. Press the roof panels on top and hold for about 1 minute, to help the roof stick. Then allow to harden for about 1 hour.

5. Once the house feels very secure, it's time to decorate the roof! Pipe icing along the bottom third of the roof. Working at the base of the roof, stick a row of cereal into the icing, slightly extending past the edge of the roof.

Place another row of cereal above, slightly overlapping the bottom row, like shingles. Continue until both roof panels are covered. Stick one final row of cereal squares on the top of the roof.

6. Use the remaining icing to fill in any blank areas, particularly at the edges of the roof panels.

7. Allow the house to harden for a final hour, then enjoy!

No-Bake Pocky "Gingerbread" House

This is way easier than it looks, and oh my, doesn't it look absolutely adorable?!

½ batch Classic Royal Icing (page 93)

Walls, Front and Back:
About 50 dark chocolate Pocky sticks
12 graham cracker squares

Door:
5 strawberry Pocky sticks
1 dark chocolate Pocky stick

Roof:
About 50 Pocky sticks, any flavor
14 graham cracker squares
2 almond Pocky sticks

Trees:
15 green tea Pocky sticks
3 dark chocolate Pocky sticks
3 marshmallows
Confectioners' sugar, for dusting

Build the Side Walls:

1. Place the Classic Royal Icing into a piping bag fitted with a medium-sized, round piping tip.

2. Pipe icing onto the bottom third of 2 attached graham cracker squares. Stick dark chocolate Pocky into the icing, alternating the direction that the Pocky is facing and allow some of the icing to squish out between each Pocky. This will make it look like a snowy log cabin!

3. Keep working in increments, adding some more icing, then sticking more Pocky to it, until the side wall is covered. We use this method because the icing dries quickly and we want the Pocky to stick.

4. Repeat with the other side wall and set these aside for the icing to harden, about 1 hour.

Build the Front and Back Wall and Door:

1. Very gently cut the corners off of two graham cracker squares to create the shape featured in the building guide. Don't worry if they break a little bit, you can use the icing to glue them back together.

2. In the same method as the side walls, add icing in increments and attach Pocky, moving upward. The graham crackers will be secured together as you add more Pocky, so don't worry about attaching them beforehand.

(Continued on page 180)

3. Once the sides begin to narrow, you will have to gently trim the Pocky before gluing it to the house.

4. Repeat with the back wall. To one wall, glue 5 pieces of strawberry Pocky into the center, as the door. Find a scrap piece of dark chocolate Pocky and glue it on with more icing, creating the door handle.

5. Set these aside and allow to harden, about 1 hour.

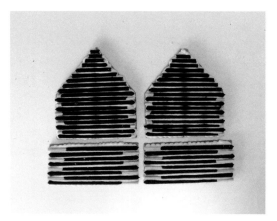

Build the Roof Panels:

1. Each roof panel consists of 1½ graham cracker squares. They will need to be connected before adding Pocky, so use some extra icing to attach extra graham cracker to the back of the roof panel, extending horizontally across all 3 panels. Be sure to center this supporting panel, as you don't want it to interfere when you're gluing the roof to the house. Then flip the panel over so that it is facing right side up.

2. Glue the Pocky vertically onto the roof. I trimmed the plain breadstick portion off each Pocky, but you don't have to! You can use one flavor of Pocky or go crazy and use everything you can find!

3. Repeat with the other roof panel and allow the icing to dry, about 1 hour.

Assembly:

1. Use the icing to glue one wall panel to the front house panel. Hold it in place for a couple seconds, then gently release and wait 10 minutes. Add the other wall panel and glue it to the front house panel. Wait 30 minutes for the icing to harden.

2. Pipe some more icing onto the open ends of the wall panels and attach the back house panel. Hold in place (or use a box of pasta—I did this!) for a couple minutes, then allow the icing to harden for about 1 hour.

3. You can also pipe additional icing along the seams of the house for extra support once they begin to stick together.

4. Once the bottom walls feel secure, pipe more icing onto the diagonal sides of the front and back panels. Press the roof panels on top and hold for about 1 minute, to help the roof stick. Then allow to harden for about 30 minutes.

5. Pipe some extra icing onto the seam between the roof panels and stick 2 almond Pocky sticks on top. Allow the house to harden for about 1 hour.

Make the Trees:

1. Trim the green tea Pocky into increasingly smaller pieces, creating 3 triangle-shaped stacks of Pocky.

2. Pipe a vertical line of icing down the center of each tree and stick a dark chocolate Pocky on top. Allow the icing to set for about 30 minutes (this oddly takes longer than most of the house).

Serve:

1. Gently place the house on your serving tray.

2. Cut the bottoms off the marshmallows to make them sticky, then stick them onto the tray. Stick the Pocky trees into the marshmallows.

3. Gently dust the confectioners' sugar over the house to look like a fresh snowfall. Enjoy!

No-Bake Cookie House

If you don't have an oven or want to use an oven, this house is for you! All you need is cookies, chocolate, and someone who loves cookies!

House:
3 cups chocolate chips, melted
20 sandwich cookies
6 graham cracker squares
10 rectangular cookies
3 (3.5-ounce) white chocolate bars
3 (3.5-ounce) dark chocolate bars
6 squares dark chocolate, intact (for the door)
Icing wreath decoration

Scenery:
2 hazelnut truffles
3 bars of dark chocolate
10 sandwich cookies
¼ cup mini chocolate chips
Confectioners' sugar, for dusting

Build the House:
1. Make 4 stacks of 5 sandwich cookies, placing a dollop of chocolate between each cookie, gluing them together. Place them on a flat tray that will easily fit into your fridge.

2. Spread some additional chocolate onto the sides of the cookie stacks and attach the graham crackers to them, creating the walls of the house, trimming if needed. If necessary, spread some chocolate between the graham crackers for additional structural support. Transfer the house to the fridge for the chocolate to set, about 20 minutes.

(Continued on page 184)

3. Use the white and dark chocolate bars to create the foundation of the roof. Start with a layer of dark chocolate that completely covers the cookie stacks and extends to the edge of the graham cracker walls. Spread some melted chocolate on top, then place a layer of white chocolate on top. It should be as long as the dark chocolate layer underneath, but slightly more narrow. Add more melted chocolate as glue, then add another dark chocolate layer, again making it as long as the white chocolate layer, but slightly more narrow. Continue until you have 3 layers of both the white and dark chocolate and you have built a pyramid shape. Place the house in the fridge for 30 minutes to chill.

4. Use some more melted chocolate to glue 5 rectangular cookies to each side of the roof. You may have to hold each cookie in place for a couple seconds for it to stick. The cool temperature of the house will help expedite this process. Then chill the house for another 15 minutes.

5. Stick the 6 intact squares of chocolate onto the front of the house with some extra melted chocolate. Then attach the icing wreath with some more melted chocolate. This will create the door! Return the house to the fridge while you set up the platter.

Decorate the Platter:

1. Place 3 dark chocolate bars flat onto your platter. This will be the ground.

2. Gently place the house on top. Place a hazelnut truffle on either side of the door and spoon the mini chocolate chips onto the platter as the cobblestone path.

3. Gently cut the remaining sandwich cookies in half and use them as the fence.

4. Lastly, dust the confectioners' sugar over the house and the platter to look like a fresh dusting of snow.

GINGERBREAD BRICK BARN

This is a mega cake, but it's also a surprise pull-apart cake! The cake is sliced into "bricks" and stacked, so guests can eat as many pieces as they like! But be sure to pull from the top and not the bottom!

Syrup:
1 cup peeled and sliced fresh ginger
1 batch Simple Syrup, still warm and in the pot (page 95)

Cake Batter:
8 cups all-purpose flour
4 teaspoons baking powder
2 teaspoons baking soda
4 teaspoons salt
2 tablespoons + 2 teaspoons ground ginger
4 teaspoons ground cinnamon
2 cups unsalted butter, room temperature
4 cups granulated sugar
4 large eggs, room temperature
3 cups molasses
2 cups milk

Frosting:
24 ounces cream cheese, room temperature
1½ cups unsalted butter, room temperature
3 teaspoons vanilla extract
10 cups confectioners' sugar
Green food coloring
Red sprinkles
2 squares graham crackers
2 cups shredded wheat cereal (e.g., Mini-Wheats)

Make the Syrup:

1. Add the sliced ginger to the Simple Syrup and set it to medium heat. Bring the syrup to a simmer, cover, and boil for 10 minutes.

2. Turn off the heat and allow the ginger to infuse in the syrup for 1 hour.

Bake the Cake:

1. Preheat the oven to 350°F. Grease two 9 × 13–inch cake pans.

2. Combine the flour, baking powder, baking soda, salt, ginger, and cinnamon in a bowl. Set aside.

3. In a large bowl, beat the butter and sugar with an electric mixer until light and fluffy. Add the eggs, molasses, and milk and beat until fully combined. Add the dry ingredients and mix until just combined.

4. Divide the batter between the cake pans and bake them for 45 to 50 minutes, until a skewer inserted into the centers comes out clean. Cool completely in the pans.

Make the Frosting:

1. Place the cream cheese and butter in a large bowl and beat with an electric mixer until pale and fluffy. Add the vanilla extract and mix to combine.

2. Add the confectioners' sugar 1 cup at a time, mixing with each addition. Then beat for another 3 minutes, until light and fluffy.

(Continued on page 186)

Assembly:

1. Use a serrated knife to cut off the crusts on all sides and flatten the tops of the cake. Generously brush the ginger syrup onto the cake and allow the syrup to soak into the cake for about 10 minutes, or until the surface feels less sticky.

2. Cut the cakes into 2-inch-wide by 12-inch-long strips. Then cut each strip into 3 bricks, making them 2 inches by 4 inches.

3. Start to stack the bricks on your platter of choice, cutting the bricks in half when necessary and spreading the frosting in between and on top of the bricks, just like you were building a brick house! Refer to the stacking guide provided and repeat the stacking pattern twice, creating 6 layers.

4. Use the remaining bricks to create a roof shape, according to the stacking guide, to create an angled roof. Use the serrated knife to smooth any edges that are sticking out.

5. Spread extra frosting onto the roof and stick the shredded wheat cereal onto the roof as shingles.

6. Use some frosting as glue to attach the graham cracker door and window to the sides of the house. Then place the frosting in a piping bag fitted with a medium, round piping tip. Pipe the details of the door and window.

7. Dye the remaining frosting green and plate it into a piping bag fitted with a medium, star-shaped piping tip. Pipe greenery onto the sides of the house and the window. Stick red sprinkles onto the greenery to look like berries.

8. Place a couple more pieces of cereal to the side of the cake to look like hay bales. Enjoy!

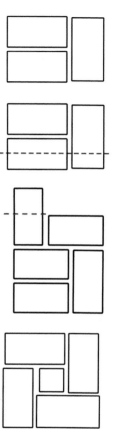

Mɪɴɪ Gɪɴɢᴇʀʙʀᴇᴀᴅ Hᴏᴜꜱᴇꜱ

MAKES ABOUT 6-8 HOUSES

1 batch Classic Gingerbread Cookies dough (page 71)
1 batch Classic Royal Icing (page 93)
Desired sprinkles or colored sugar

Bake:

1. Preheat the oven to 350°F. Line a baking sheet with parchment paper.

2. Roll the dough out on a floured surface until it is ⅛-inch thick. Using the image below as a guide, make paper templates of each wall and cut out two house "fronts," two "walls," and two "roofs" for each house. Transfer the cookies to the baking sheet, then chill them in the fridge for 10 minutes. This will prevent them from spreading too much while in the oven.

3. Bake the cookies at for about 10 minutes, until the edges begin to darken. Transfer the cookies to a wire rack and cool completely.

Build the Houses:

1. Place the Classic Royal Icing into a piping bag fitted with a small, round piping tip.

2. Glue the two walls to one "front" of the house first and wait about 10 minutes for the icing the harden. Then attach the other "front" of the house with some more icing and wait 15 minutes. Pipe more icing onto the diagonal edges of the front and back of the houses and attach the roof panels. Allow the icing to fully harden, about 1 hour.

3. Decorate the houses as you like, piping scallops or stripes on the roof, borders around the doors, or polka dots everywhere else! Allow the icing to fully set before eating or using to decorate your other baked treats.

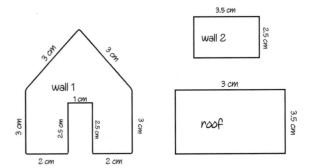

ALL-PINK GINGERBREAD HOUSE

This gingerbread house is actually made of sugar cookie dough, so if you know someone who loves the holidays but doesn't love gingerbread, this house is perfect for them! And if you love pink, this house is perfect for you, too!

Cookie Dough:
4 cups all-purpose flour
½ teaspoon salt
1 teaspoon baking powder
1 cup unsalted butter, room temperature
2 cups granulated sugar
¼ cup milk
2 large eggs, room temperature
1 teaspoon vanilla extract
Pink food coloring

Decorations:
1 batch Classic Royal Icing (page 93)
Green food coloring
⅓ cup ruby chocolate, roughly chopped
½ cup red and pink soft candy squares
Metallic sprinkles
Mini marshmallows
Pink sanding sugar

Bake the House:

1. Combine the flour, salt, and baking powder in a bowl. In a separate bowl, cream the butter and sugar with an electric mixer until it becomes light and fluffy. Add the milk, eggs, vanilla extract, and pink food coloring and mix well. Slowly add the flour mixture and mix until just combined.

2. Divide the dough into 2 balls and wrap it in plastic wrap. Chill it in the fridge for 1 hour, or until firm.

3. Roll the dough out on a floured surface to ¼-inch thick. Follow the guide provided (on page 174) to measure out the front, back, 2 sides, and 2 roof panels of the house.

(Continued on page 192)

4. Place the cookies on 2 baking sheets lined with parchment paper. Place the baking sheets in the fridge for about 15 minutes, for the cookies to stiffen. This will prevent the cookies from spreading and becoming misshapen while baking.

5. Bake the cookies for 15 to 18 minutes, until the edges begin to darken. Allow the cookies to cool completely on the baking sheets so that they stay flat.

Decorate:
1. Place the Classic Royal Icing into a piping bag fitted with a small, round piping tip.

2. Pipe the foundational parts of the decorating first—the stripes, the windows, etc.

3. To create the cobblestone effect, pipe some icing onto the house and press pieces of ruby chocolate into it. Work in increments and extending it along the bottom of all the wall panels, leaving room for the chimney.

4. To make the chimney, cut the red and pink candy squares in half, creating little bricks. Glue them to the back wall of the house in a chimney shape, piping some icing between each brick as well, to make it look realistic.

5. Dye some of the icing a vibrant green color, place it in a piping bag fitted with a small, round piping tip and pipe a garland on the front of the house and some greenery under the windows. Add little sprinkles to the garland as ornaments.

6. To make the door, I used a knife to spread a thin layer of white icing into a curved rectangular shape, then allowed it to dry. I used the same icing and a piping bag fitted with a small, round piping tip to pipe the border of the door and the three panels. I used a sprinkle for the door handle.

7. For the roof, pipe a crosshatch pattern using the icing by piping a series of diagonal lines in one direction, then another series of lines in another direction on top. Pour the pink sanding sugar onto a baking sheet and press the roof panel on top, sticking the sugar to the icing.

8. Allow the icing to harden, about 2 hours.

Assembly:
1. Use the icing to glue one wall panel to the front house panel. Hold it in place for a couple seconds, then gently release and wait 10 minutes. Add the other wall panel and glue it to the front house panel. Wait 30 minutes for the icing to harden.

2. Pipe some more icing onto the open ends of the wall panels and attach the back house panel. Hold in place for a couple minutes, then allow the icing to harden for about 1 hour.

3. You can also pipe additional icing along the seams of the house for extra support once they begin to stick together.

4. Once the bottom walls feel secure, pipe more icing onto the diagonal sides of the front and back panels. Press the roof panels on top and hold for about 1 minute to help the roof stick. Then allow to harden for about 1 hour.

5. Place the remaining icing into a piping bag fitted with a medium-sized star-shaped piping tip. Pipe dollops onto the seam of the roof and decorate with mini marshmallows and sprinkles.

6. Use the remaining icing to fill in any blank areas, particularly at the edges of the roof panels.

7. Allow the house to harden for 1 more hour, then enjoy!

CHARCUTERIE CHALET

If you've had your fill of gingerbread, here is a savory house to enjoy! I recommend serving this with crackers, green grapes, and your favorite holiday movie.

Filling:
14 ounces cheese, room temperature
2¼ cups cream cheese, room temperature
2½ cups grated cheddar cheese, room temperature
Pinch of pepper
1 pepperoni stick
10–20 grissini sticks, depending on the thickness
½ cup white cheddar cubes (1 cm)
½ cup orange cheddar cubes (1 cm)
24 slices of pepperoni
1 (1- × 2-inch) rectangle white cheddar cheese
2 tablespoons shelled pistachios
¼ cup finely chopped pecans
⅓ cup grated Parmesan cheese
3 mini cheese rounds (Brie, mozzarella— whatever you like!)
Rosemary and thyme sprigs

Make the Filling:

1. Place the goat cheese and cream cheese in a bowl and beat with an electric mixer until smooth. Add the grated cheddar cheese and pepper and mix until combined.

2. Place this on a large sheet of plastic wrap and shape into a house shape, including a pointed roof. Set aside about ¼ cup of filling.

3. Wrap the house in plastic wrap and chill in the fridge for 30 minutes.

Assembly:

1. Spread the remaining filling onto your serving platter. Sprinkle the Parmesan cheese on top to look like snow. Stick the house on top.

2. Press the grissini sticks onto the two longer sides of the house.

3. Cut the white and orange cheddar cubes in half, creating 1- by ½-centimeter cheese bricks. Stick these bricks to the shorter sides of the house, extending all the way up to the roof.

4. Use the slices of pepperoni as shingles, starting from the base of the roof and working upward.

5. Trim the ends off the pepperoni stick and place the stick at the top of the roof.

6. Use the offcuts of the pepperoni stick to create a doorhandle and stick it to the rectangle of white cheddar cheese. Stick the door to one of the sides with the grissini sticks.

7. Place the pistachios around the edge of the house and sprinkle the pecans onto the platter as the path. Place the cheese rounds around the house and stick fresh rosemary into them, creating trees! Use the thyme sprigs as little accents of greenery around the edges of the house.

GINGERBREAD GREENHOUSE

I love this house. I love this house so much. Not only is the gingerbread absolutely delicious and fragrant, but it also acts as a beautiful, glowing centerpiece for any holiday party or dinner table! Because of the addition of rosemary, it will also be at home on the table while you serve Christmas dinner.

1 batch Classic Gingerbread Cookies dough
   (page 71)
1 batch Classic Royal Icing (page 93)
7–8 gelatin sheets
5 marshmallows
Fresh rosemary sprigs
Tiny, battery-powered fairy lights

Bake the Walls:

1. Preheat the oven to 350°F.

2. Roll the dough out on a floured surface to ¼-inch thick. Follow the guide provided (on page 174) to measure out the front, back, 2 sides, and 2 roof panels of the house.

3. Place the cookies on 2 baking sheets lined with parchment paper. Place the baking sheets in the fridge for about 15 minutes, for the cookies to stiffen. Use a very sharp knife to cut out the windows and door panels. I created the door from one of the window panels that I cut out! This is delicate work, but working with chilled dough will make it so much easier.

4. Place the baking sheets in the freezer (if they can fit) or the fridge for about 30 minutes. This will prevent the cookies from spreading and becoming misshapen while baking, which is especially important for this house, as it will be extra noticeable.

5. Bake the cookies for 12 to 15 minutes, until the edges begin to darken. Allow the cookies to cool completely on the baking sheets, so that they stay flat.

(Continued on page 198)

Decorate:

1. Place the Classic Royal Icing into a piping bag fitted with a small, round piping tip.

2. Flip the cookies over so that the bottoms of the cookies are facing up. Use scissors to cut squares from the gelatin sheets and attach them to the windows, using the icing as glue. As soon as a wall panel has its windows attached, flip it right-side up on the baking sheet so that the weight of the cookie will prevent the edges of the gelatin from curling while it dries.

 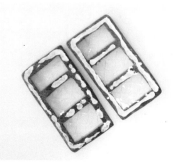 

3. Keeping the cookies flat on the baking sheets, pipe straight borders around the edges of wall panels and the windows. Simple, but beautiful! Allow the icing to harden, about 2 hours.

Assembly:

1. Use the icing to glue one wall panel to the front house panel. Hold it in place for a couple seconds, then gently release and wait 10 minutes. Add the other wall panel and glue it to the front house panel. Wait 30 minutes for the icing to harden.

2. Pipe some more icing onto the open ends of the wall panels and attach the back house panel. Hold in place for a couple minutes, then allow the icing to harden for about 1 hour.

3. You can also pipe additional icing along the seams of the house for extra support once they begin to stick together.

4. Once the bottom walls feel secure, pipe more icing onto the diagonal sides of the front and back panels. Press one roof panel on top and hold for about 1 minute, to help the roof stick. Then allow to harden for about 1 hour.

5. Glue the door to the outside of the greenhouse, leaving it slightly ajar. You might have to stick a couple cookies under the door to support it while it dries.

6. Once the house feels very secure, it's time to fill the greenhouse! Cut the marshmallows in half with scissors and use the sticky side to stick the marshmallows on the "floor" inside the house. Stick the fresh rosemary sprigs into the marshmallows. Gently place the fairy lights inside the house, feeding the cord out through one bottom corner of the roof. Make sure that you don't leave the on/off switch inside the house!

7. Glue the remaining roof panel onto the house.

8. Use the remaining icing to fill in any blank areas, particularly at the edges of the roof panels.

9. Allow the house to harden for 1 hour, then turn on the fairy lights and enjoy!

GINGERBREAD HOUSE MOUSSE CAKE

MAKES 1 (9-INCH) CAKE

The most wildly adorable cake and a fun twist on a classic gingerbread house! The milk chocolate mousse is so creamy, you'll be in love. If you prefer dark chocolate, you can absolutely use that instead!

1½ recipe Classic Gingerbread Cookies
   dough (page 71)
1 recipe Classic Royal Icing (page 93)
Colored sanding sugar

Cake base:
⅔ cup all-purpose flour
⅓ cup cocoa powder
1 teaspoon ground cinnamon
⅔ cup sugar
¾ teaspoon baking soda
¾ teaspoon baking powder
¼ teaspoon salt
1 large egg
¼ cup milk
3 tablespoons oil
½ teaspoon vanilla extract
¼ cup water

Mousse Filling:
4 teaspoons powdered gelatin
¼ cup cold water
6 large egg whites
2 cups whipping cream
1¼ cups good-quality milk chocolate
⅔ cup milk

Make the Cookie Houses:

1. Preheat the oven to 350°F.

2. Roll the cookie dough out on a floured surface to ¼ inch thick.

3. Cut long strips of dough. The length isn't important, but the width is! This is because the houses can be of varying heights, but you need a specific width of houses to fit around the circumference of the cake. You will need:
   - two 4-inch-wide strips
   - two 3.5-inch-wide strips
   - five 3-inch-wide strips

4. Use a sharp knife to cut the houses (and their pointed roofs) to your desired height. A variety different house heights will look best.

5. Place the cookies on a baking sheet and bake for 12 minutes, or until the edges of the cookies are starting to brown. Cool completely.

6. To decorate, place the Classic Royal Icing in a piping bag fitted with a small, round piping tip. Start with any features you'd like to dip in sugar. You can do this by piping a roof, wreath, bushes, etc. with icing, then dipping the cookie directly into colored sugar.

(Continued on page 202)

7. Then pipe on the remaining accents to the houses. I found that piping a border around the houses added a very cute finishing touch to the houses.

8. Allow the icing to dry at room temperature while you bake the cake.

Bake the Cake:

1. Preheat the oven to 350°F.

2. Place the flour, cocoa powder, cinnamon, sugar, baking soda, baking powder, and salt in the bowl of an electric mixer and mix on low speed until fully combined. Add the egg, milk, oil, vanilla, and water and mix until smooth.

3. Line the sides and bottom of a 9-inch springform pan with parchment paper and pour the batter into the pan. Bake for 20 to 30 minutes, or until a skewer inserted into the center comes out clean.

4. Place the pan on a cooling rack and cool completely in the pan.

5. Remove the cake from the pan and remove the parchment paper lining. Return the cake to the pan and set aside.

Make the Mousse:

1. Sprinkle the gelatin into the cold water and set aside.

2. Beat the egg whites until stiff peaks form. In a separate bowl, beat the whipping cream until soft peaks form and set both bowls aside.

3. Set a small saucepan to medium heat and add the milk. Just before the milk comes to a boil, turn off the heat and add the gelatin. Once the gelatin has fully dissolved, add the milk chocolate, and whisk until fully melted. You may need to turn the heat back on to fully melt the chocolate. Add this mixture to the whipped cream and whisk to combine.

4. Then add the egg whites and whisk to combine, making sure to keep the mixture as airy as possible.

5. Pour the mousse on top of the chocolate cake and smooth the surface. Transfer the cake to the fridge to set for 6 hours or overnight.

Assembly:

1. Run a sharp knife along the inside of the springform pan to detach the cake from the pan. Unlatch the sides of the pan and carefully remove it.

2. Place the cake on your serving platter and gently stick the gingerbread houses to the sides of the cake. The mousse should be sticky enough to hold up the houses. Slice and enjoy!

Acknowledgments

Firstly, I want to thank *you*! My wonderful readers, subscribers, and followers. The only reason that I've had the opportunity to write these books is because of your support and enthusiasm for my recipes and content, and I am incredibly grateful for every single like, comment, and follow. I've been able to create my dream job because of you, and I feel so fortunate. I hope to continue to bring you happiness through my food and creativity!

I also want to thank my wonderful editor, Nicole Frail, for putting this entire book together! The amount of work that it takes to turn my photos and typed recipes into a fully fledged book is so overwhelming, and I appreciate her enthusiasm, support, and massive amount of hard work.

Thank you to my wonderful boyfriend, Brendan, whose level of support and encouragement has been otherworldly. From taking time out of his day to brainstorm ideas with me, bringing me snacks and helping with recipe prep on shoot days, and believing in me and my dreams when I felt unsure of myself—I have never felt so lucky and cared for. Thank you for cleaning my stove when the cherry syrup from the Snowy Forest Cabin Cake overflowed and for buying me mashed potatoes and massaging my hands after I submitted the manuscript. You make all of my dreams feel possible. I love you.

Lastly, thank you to my doggies, Paddington and Treacle, for ensuring my floors stayed clean and crumb free. Their determination to catch scraps before they even had a chance to hit the floor provided constant entertainment on stressful days! Treacle was the boldest one for a change, sneakily licking the Gingerbread Breakfast Muffins while I changed the lens on my camera. I hope you enjoyed those flavors, Treacle, because next time I'll be more vigilant!

INDEX

METRIC CONVERSIONS

If you're accustomed to using metric measurements, use these handy charts to convert the imperial measurements used in this book.

Weight (Dry Ingredients)

1 oz		30 g
4 oz	¼ lb	120 g
8 oz	½ lb	240 g
12 oz	¾ lb	360 g
16 oz	1 lb	480 g
32 oz	2 lb	960 g

Oven Temperatures

Fahrenheit	Celsius	Gas Mark
225°	110°	¼
250°	120°	½
275°	140°	1
300°	150°	2
325°	160°	3
350°	180°	4
375°	190°	5
400°	200°	6
425°	220°	7
450°	230°	8

Volume (Liquid Ingredients)

½ tsp.		2 ml
1 tsp.		5 ml
1 Tbsp.	½ fl oz	15 ml
2 Tbsp.	1 fl oz	30 ml
¼ cup	2 fl oz	60 ml
⅓ cup	3 fl oz	80 ml
½ cup	4 fl oz	120 ml
⅔ cup	5 fl oz	160 ml
¾ cup	6 fl oz	180 ml
1 cup	8 fl oz	240 ml
1 pt	16 fl oz	480 ml
1 qt	32 fl oz	960 ml

Length

¼ in	6 mm
½ in	13 mm
¾ in	19 mm
1 in	25 mm
6 in	15 cm
12 in	30 cm

ALSO AVAILABLE

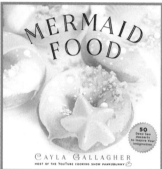